Checked 4/11/11

Please renew/return this item by the last

So that your telephone call is charged at
please call the numbers as set out below.

	From Area codes 01923 or 020:	From the r
Renewals:	01923 471373	01438 737
Enquiries:	01923 471333	01438 737
Textphone:	01923 471599	01438 7375

L32   www.hertsdirect.org/librarycatalo

SPRITES & MIDGETS

Other Titles in the Crowood AutoClassics Series

Ferrari Dino	Anthony Curtis
Jaguar E-type	Jonathan Wood
MGB	Brian Laban
Porsche 911	David Vivian
Lamborghini Countach	Peter Dron
Lotus Elan	Mike Taylor
Triumph TRs	Graham Robson
AC Cobra	Brian Laban
Lotus Esprit	Jeremy Walton
Jensen Interceptor	John Tipler

SPRITES & MIDGETS

The Complete Story

Anders Ditlev Clausager

CROWOOD
AUTOCLASSICS

First published in 1991 by
The Crowood Press Ltd
Ramsbury, Marlborough
Wiltshire SN8 2HR

British Library Cataloguing in Publication Data

Clausager, Anders Ditlev *1949–*
   Sprites & Midgets.
   1. Cars. History
   I. Title
   629.2222

ISBN   1 85223 509 8

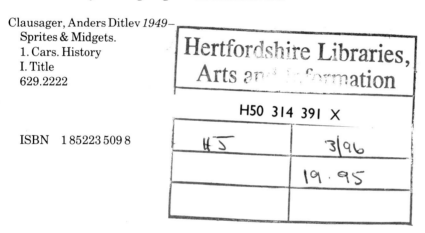

The majority of the photographs in this book were kindly supplied
by The Motoring Picture Library, Beaulieu.
   The line drawing on page 32 was drawn by Bob Constant. All
other line drawings are reproduced courtesy of the British Motor
Industry Heritage Trust (Rover Group), as are the photographs on
pages 19 (bottom), 25 (bottom), 147 (bottom), 149 and 150.

Typeset by Acorn Bookwork, Salisbury, Wiltshire
Printed in England by Richard Clay Ltd

Contents

Life and Times of the Spridget

1923   The first MG cars are made.

1928   The first MG Midget, the M-type, is introduced at the London Motor Show.

1929   The MG factory moves to Abingdon-on-Thames.

1935   MG becomes part of the Nuffield organization.

1946   The Healey company is formed, and the first Healey car built.

1952   *April*   Nuffield and Austin join forces as the British Motor Corporation.
October   The first Austin-Healey is introduced.

1955   The last of the classic MG Midgets, the TF model, is discontinued.

1956   Donald and Geoffrey Healey begin to design the Sprite.

1957   The first prototype Sprite is shown to BMC, and approved for production. Austin-Healey production moves from Longbridge to the MG factory at Abingdon.

1958   *March*   The Sprite goes into production at Abingdon.
May   Public launch of the Sprite.
July   First rally appearance for the Sprite, in the Alpine rally.

1959   *March*   First major race appearance for the Sprite at Sebring, USA. A Sprite also appears in the Targa Florio for the first time. EX.219, a Sprite-engined version of the MG record car EX.179, sets a number of international class G records on the Bonneville Salt Flats, Utah, USA.
March   The Austin-Healey 3000 is launched.
The Healeys design the Coventry Climax engined 'Super Sprite'.
September   First Sprite CKD kits are shipped to Australia for local assembly.

1960   *June*   A Sprite runs for the first time in the Le Mans 24-hour race.
November   The Sprite-based Innocenti Spyder is introduced in Italy.
December   Production of the Sprite Mark I ceases, with the exception of CKD kits.

1961   *March*   Production of the Sprite Mark II and Midget Mark I starts.
May   Public launch of the Sprite Mark II.
June   Public launch of the Midget Mark I.
November   Rally debut for the Midget, with a class win in the RAC rally.

1962   *March*   The Sprite Mark II enters its first major race, at Sebring.
May   Dick Jacobs begins to race his two special Midget coupes.
October   Sprite/Midget 1,098cc models with front disc brakes are introduced.
Another new model from BMC at the London Motor Show is the first MGB. Also at this time, Triumph launch their Spridget competitor, the Spitfire.

1963   In the USA, Donna Mae Mims wins the SCCA class H National Championship in her pink Sprite.

1964   BMC finalize design of the ADO34/ADO35, a front-wheel-drive Spridget replacement with Pininfarina bodywork, but this is eventually shelved.
March   Sprite Mark III/Midget Mark II introduced, with improved 1,098cc engine, semi-elliptic rear springs, wind-down windows and new dashboard.

1965	The Healeys design 'WAEC', a mid-engined Spridget replacement proposal, but this is not adopted by BMC for production.
1966	*October* Sprite Mark IV/Midget Mark III introduced with 1,275cc engine and convertible-type hood.
1967	Small numbers of Sprites and Midgets are built at Cowley rather than Abingdon. *November* North American Spridget export models are now fitted with the first emissions control engine, a new padded dashboard and dual circuit brakes, to comply with the forthcoming 1968 US legislation.
1968	*January* The merger between BMC and Leyland is announced. *March* The last Austin-Healey 3000 is manufactured. During 1968, the works Sprite racing cars make their final appearances at Sebring, Le Mans and the Nürburgring. *November* John Sprinzel enters a Midget in the London to Sydney marathon rally.
1969	*March* Final appearance of a Sprite at Sebring. The Sprite is withdrawn from North American and other export markets. *October* 1970 model Spridgets feature Rostyle wheels, black sills, new black grilles, rear quarter bumpers and new style seat trim.
1970	Donald Stokes of BLMC cancels the contract to use the Healey name.
1971	*January* The Austin-Healey Sprite becomes the Austin Sprite. *July* The Sprite is discontinued. *August* The 1972 model MG Midget features round rear wheelarches, the first of the 12V type engines, and new Rostyle wheels like the MGB.
1972	*December* The Midget is fitted with an alternator in place of the dynamo.
1973	The Midget is now marketed only in the UK and in North America.
1974	The Midget Mark III chrome bumper model is replaced by the Midget 1500, with a Triumph Spitfire type engine, all-synchromesh Triumph/Morris Marina gearbox, an anti-roll bar and rubber bumpers.
1975	The Midget 1500 is introduced in the Californian market, fitted with an engine adapted to use lead-free fuel, and a catalyst exhaust.
1976	For the 1977 model year, Midgets for other North American markets are fitted with the leadfree-tolerant engine and catalyst.
1977	Head-rests and inertia reel seat-belts become standard fittings on home market cars.
1978	Console with radio speaker fitted as standard, together with an aerial. Dual circuit braking system introduced also for home market cars.
1979	*September* Abingdon celebrates the 50th anniversary of the MG factory. In the following week, BL announce that the factory will be closed, and that the MG Midget and MGB models will be discontinued. *November* Production of the Midget ceases. The final run of 500 home market cars are all painted black, and are supplied with a special badge commemorating fifty years of the MG Midget.

The 1966 Sprite brochure. Presumably the setting is seventh heaven rather than Cloud-cuckoo-land.

The interior of the Sprite Mark IV, from a 1966 brochure.

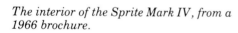

The original MG Midget sales brochure with the famous 'Safety fast!' motto on the front cover.

1980   It is still possible to buy a new Midget, from dealers' stocks of unregistered cars . . .
August   Production of the Triumph Spitfire ceases.
October   Production of the MGB ceases.

1981   And there are still some 'new' Midgets available in the UK . . .
January   Launch of the final MGB model, the 'Limited Edition'.
The Abingdon factory is closed.

1982   The first new-generation MG, the MG Metro, is introduced, followed by the MG Metro Turbo.

1983   Second new MG, the Maestro 1600.

1984   Third new MG, the Montego fuel-injected 2-litre saloon.

1985   The MG Maestro is fitted with the 2-litre fuel injection engine.

1986   Graham Day arrives as chairman of BL, and the company is renamed Rover Group.

1987   Speculation grows that there might be a new MG sports car in the future.

1988   The Rover Group is taken over by British Aerospace.

1989   The new Rover 200-series is launched; industry commentators predict a new MG sports car, using the 200-series floorpan and engines.

1990   While we are still waiting for the new MG, the Frogeye Car Company in the Isle of Wight brings back the original Sprite, with a glassfibre body, a 1,275cc engine and a price tag of £14,000.

1991   We are still waiting for that new MG . . .

Introduction

The Austin-Healey Sprite and the MG Midget, long since collectively known as 'Spridgets', have quite possibly provided more enthusiasts with more fun for less money than any other sports car ever. The philosophy behind the original Sprite project, initiated in 1956, was simple: to build a low-cost sports car around standard components. Over the twenty-one year production period this principle was never departed from. Even today, more than ten years after the last MG Midget rolled off the assembly line at Abingdon, Spridgets continue to provide enjoyment for a modest outlay.

It is true that in its later years, especially after the introduction of the rubber bumper model in 1974, the MG Midget was increasingly frequently criticized for being unsophisticated and out-of-date, yet it continued to sell well because it was so much more affordable than its competitors. BMC or British Leyland could easily have brought out a really modern small sports car (if they had had the money to invest!) but any replacement model for the Spridget, while undoubtedly in absolute terms a much better car, would have been very expensive in comparison. It is significant that there has not been a really cheap small sports car since the demise of the MG Midget in 1979. Most of the present-day offerings which may lay claim to having inherited the Spridget's mantle are around twice as expensive, if we translate the original cost of the Spridgets into modern equivalent prices.

A great part of the appeal of the Spridgets lie in their affordability and their low running costs. In the case of the original Frog-eye Sprite Mark I of 1958–1961, this is coupled with the car's unique looks. (These were not always appreciated when new, but are today regarded as 'cute'.) Because the later models look so much more ordinary, they have yet to reach the same status of classic cars, while the final rubber-bumper Midget of 1974–1979 is still looked at somewhat askance. The Spridgets have a number of other common characteristics. They are all modest if willing performers, although they can be transformed into surprisingly fast cars for their size – the BMC A-series engine being a favourite subject for tuners and improvers. In mechanical terms, the Spridgets are fundamentally simple and robust. The same cannot in all honesty be said for their bodywork: simple, yes; robust, in a sense; but inevitably prone to rust! Finally, they are all of them good-natured little cars, easy to drive, with good road manners; their controls a pleasure to use.

THE MEN BEHIND THE SPRIDGET

We owe the Spridget concept and design to the calculation of Len Lord, BMC's chairman of the 1950s; the inspiration of Donald Healey, one of Britain's great sports car designers; and, not least, to the perspiration of Geoffrey Healey, Donald's son, who more than anybody else was involved in the construction of the original Frog-eye as well as many of its subsequent derivatives. But there are many others to whom to pay tribute, in particular the inspired double act of John Thornley and Syd Enever. Known respectively as Mr MG and Mr MG of Abingdon, they were responsible for producing Spridgets in such large numbers and for

This very original-looking Frog-eye Sprite is finished in Leaf Green, with the interior trim in dark green; a colour scheme which shows off well the simple, unadorned lines of the car.

The Sprite arrow badge was found on the rear of the Frog-eye.

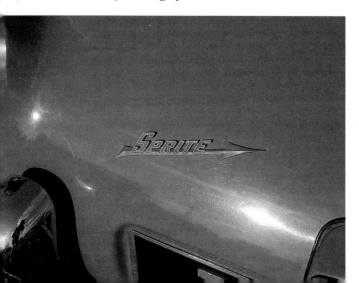

much of the development work carried out in the Spridget's heyday in the 1960s.

Only BMC could have done it. In its day the greatest British motor manufacturer, with a market share close to forty per cent, BMC's twin sports car makes of MG and Austin-Healey dominated their market, in Britain and abroad. Only BMC had the resources, the off-the-shelf components, the sales network – and the courage – to make a success of the small sports car. The Spridgets could never have been successfully made and marketed by a small concern. Many tried, but the only serious competitor for the Spridget came

from another large corporation, in the shape of Triumph's Spitfire. When the giant BMC was finally revealed to have feet of clay, it was ironic that it should merge with the Spitfire's sponsors, the Leyland Motor Corporation.

Because of the fate of the parent company, the Spridgets' glorious years were from 1958 to 1969. The final ten years of their history make sadder reading. So, for that matter,

'When skies are grey, you're still smiling . . .' The face of the Frog-eye is as cheerful as its personality.

The 1960s chrome-bumper Midget is to many people the most attractive of the later Spridget models, especially when fitted with the optional wire wheels seen on this 1965 car in Old English White.

does the history of British Leyland as a whole during those catastrophic 1970s. It was a long time before any signs of renaissance appeared in the company, and when they did, time had run out for the Spridgets. The Midget was overdue for discontinuation in 1979, and yet its demise left a gap in the sports car market, made even larger when the MGB went out of production a year later.

For more than a decade, enthusiasts have waited patiently and hopefully for a return of the MG sports car. If the gossip and rumours purveyed by motoring magazines are to be believed, they will be rewarded some time during the 1990s – although those who hope for a spiritual successor to the Spridgets are likely to be disappointed. Any new MG sports car from the present-day Rover Group is more likely to be in the MGB class, somewhat above the bargain-basement level of the original Spridget. It would obviously be too much to hope for a revival of the Austin-Healey name . . . although those who wish to do so can now buy a modern version of the original Frog-eye. Its price, however, ensures that it will mainly find a clientele among those who wish to relive their youth, or those with a fashionable desire to indulge in nostalgia.

Luckily however, there are still thousands and thousands of the original Spridgets around to ensure low-cost motoring fun and an affordable introduction to classic sports cars for a new generation of enthusiasts. And isn't that what the Spridgets were all about in the first place?

1 The Family Tree of Austin, Healey and MG

Of the three family names that were united to give birth to the Sprite and Midget, Austin was the oldest but also the one which had the least in the way of a sporting heritage. Herbert Austin (1866–1941; created Lord Austin in 1936) had been the general manager of the Wolseley company in Birmingham, where he built the first Wolseley three-wheeled car in 1896. In 1901, the original Wolseley Sheep-Shearing Company Limited sold its car-making interests to armaments group Vickers. The latter formed the new Wolseley Tool and Motor Car Company Limited, with a factory at Adderley Park alongside the Birmingham–Coventry railway. Herbert Austin continued to work for Wolseley until 1905 and developed a series of racing cars which – without much success – contested the Paris-Madrid road race, and the Gordon Bennett races.

There was, however, increasing disagreement between the Vickers directors and Austin over the matter of design. Austin stuck to an increasingly outmoded concept of transverse, horizontal engines, while the Vickers people wanted in-line vertical engines. They did, indeed, bring in precisely such a design by John Davenport Siddeley, based on the French Peugeot.

THE AUSTIN COMPANY

The upshot was that Austin decided to leave Wolseley in 1905. With backing from friends such as Frank Kayser (the Sheffield steel magnate) and the du Cros family of Dunlop,

Austin proposed to start his own company, making cars under his own name. He found a suitable site south of Birmingham, at Long-bridge in the parish of Northfield where the river Rea runs close under the Lickey hills. A disused printing work, the site lay at the junction of the main road and railway lines, and there was plenty of room for expansion in this still rural area. Although it is no longer the Austin sign that greets you at the factory gate, Longbridge remains to this day one of the most important car factories in Britain: the hub of the Rover Group.

The first Austin car took to the road in 1906. Curiously enough this was a conventional vertical-engined design, so perhaps there were other reasons for Austin's departure from Wolseley than a mere quarrel over design!

In 1908, the young company built four six-cylinder racing cars to contest the French Grand Prix at Dieppe. Two of these finished, but well down the list. Other than this one excursion, Austin mostly stayed out of motor sport. The early Austins were mostly large cars, aimed at the limited but wealthy car-buying clientele of Edwardian times.

The company's first small car, developed and manufactured jointly with the Swift company in Coventry, was a single-cylinder 7hp model of 1910. Sometimes referred to as 'The first Austin Seven', it had only this name in common with its much more famous successor.

After World War I, Austin embarked on a one-model policy for a time. The Twenty, however, was too large and expensive for the popular market and, in consequence, the Austin company came close to bankruptcy. The company was reconstructed and two new models were introduced – the Austin Twelve (or 'Heavy Twelve') and, in 1922, the Austin Seven.

THE AUSTIN SEVEN

The Seven was an almost revolutionary small car, powered by 750cc four-cylinder water-cooled engine, where many contemporary small cars (the so-called 'cyclecars') had air-cooled two-cylinder engines of larger capacity. The Seven had been designed on Herbert Austin's personal initiative, outside the company. Austin worked at home, Lickey Grange, assisted only by a junior draughtsman, eighteen-year old Stanley Edge (1903–1990). Only when all the drawings were prepared – so legend has it, using the billiards table – did Edge return to Longbridge to assist in building the first prototypes. These were ready by Whitsun 1922, although it was only by thc spring of 1923 that Sevens began to be made in substantial numbers.

Although purely conceived as an affordable car for everyman (in Herbert Austin's own words, the Seven would '...knock the motor cycle and sidecar into a cocked hat and far surpass them in comfort and passenger-carrying capacity'), it was soon discovered that it had potential as a sports car as well. Among its early successes must be mentioned its performance in the Italian cyclecar Grand Prix at Monza in May 1923. There, a tuned Seven with a lightweight body won at an average of 57mph (90kph), in the hands of Captain Arthur Waite, Herbert Austin's son-in-law. A sports model was added to the catalogue in 1924 but, as Austin Sevens were developed over the years, the highly-specialized racing cars became very different to the catalogued sports models. The racing models culminated with Murray Jamieson's amazing twin overhead camshaft single-

seaters of 1936–1939. These had supercharged engines developing up to 116bhp, and were alleged to have cost £20,000 each.

THE NIPPY

At the same time, the only remaining Seven sports model available to the public was the Nippy (originally known as the 65 model), made from 1933 to 1937. This was a comparatively tame affair, with a mildly-tuned engine just about capable of reaching the 65mph (100kph) indicated by its name, and originally cost £148. Nevertheless, it was a smart-looking little car with its helmet-type wings and well-rounded tail. Surviving production figures show that Austin only sold around 200 of this type per year. While it was not, therefore, anywhere near as popular as its remote descendant, the Austin-Healey Sprite, it is of historical interest to note that

The 1935 Austin Nippy was more advanced than the Frog-eye, at least by virtue of its opening boot-lid!

The simple dashboard of the Nippy was well stocked with instruments – a rev counter being the most noticeable omission on a sports model.

With its compact dimensions and rounded tail, the Austin Nippy does have a family resemblance to its remote descendant, the Austin-Healey Sprite Frog-eye.

the Nippy was the last small Austin sports car before the advent of the Sprite some twenty-one years later.

During the 1930s, Austin successfully established itself as one of the two leading British car manufacturers, forever in competition with their great rival, Morris. The Austin image was of conservative, well-built, reliable, but rather stolid cars. The company's slogan, 'You Invest in an Austin', was well-chosen. But despite the racing cars, and despite the Nippy and a few other sports models, nobody really thought of Austin as a sports car manufacturer.

LEN LORD

In 1938, Len Lord, formerly the vice-chairman of Morris Motors Limited, joined Austin as general manager. It soon became apparent, however, that he was Lord Austin's designated heir. In characteristic fashion, he set about revamping the company's model range and production facilities. It was probably no coincidence that the Austin Seven – after seventeen years and a production run of almost 290,000 cars – was pensioned off at the beginning of 1939. Its replacement was a much more effective competitor for new Morris and Ford models. It was the Lord-inspired Austin Eight.

Lord's initial momentum was halted on the outbreak of war. Lord Austin died in 1941, and E L Payton, who had become the company's chairman, resigned owing to bad health in 1945. So Lord, in turn, became chairman and sole managing director. The early post-war Austin cars – the A40, A70 and A125 models – were far more modern in design, but were still aimed at the mainstream middle-class family car market. Only when Lord became interested in building more specialized cars for export did Austin once again develop more sporting models. However, their first such experiments were rather pathetic. The A90 Atlantic was a

powerful four-seater convertible incorporating such novelties as a hydraulic hood, hydraulic windows, and a radio. Introduced in 1948, it was a disaster in its intended market, the USA, where only 350 (of a total production run of 7,981 cars) were sold. It had disappeared by 1952. Then, there was the A40 Sports model, using the A40 Devon saloon chassis, with a tuned engine and another four-seater body, built by Jensen under contract. This was even less popular, and total production amounted to only 4,011 cars over the years 1950–1953.

THE 'NEW SEVEN'

The pre-war type Austin Eight was discontinued in 1947, and there was no new small car in the first post-war generation of Austin cars. Only in the 1951 Motor Show did Austin reveal a new small car. This was the A30, at first christened the 'New Seven' in memory of its famous forebear. Although never as good a car as its eternal rival, the Morris Minor, the A30 was nevertheless a most important car in Austin history, and together with its immediate A35 descendants would reach a total production of almost 578,000 cars until the last van derivative was discontinued in 1968. The A30 was the first Austin to use a unitary construction body. It was the first car to use the BMC A-series engine, originally of 803cc. As we shall see, the A30/35 model range had a most important part to play in the story of the Sprite and Midget.

In 1952, Lord achieved his supreme triumph when the Austin company merged with the Nuffield Organization (embracing Morris, MG, Riley and Wolseley). Even after the merger, the long-standing rivalry between Austin and Nuffield continued. Lord was especially keen on Austin having its own sports car to rival Nuffield's successful MG, particularly in lucrative overseas markets such as the USA. Then, in the 1952 Motor Show, he found exactly the sort of car he

Many of the mechanical components of the Sprite were borrowed from Austin's small car of the 1950s, the A35 model.

The contemporary Morris rival, the Minor 1000, also contributed to the new small Austin-Healey model.

wanted ... and he found a man he could do business with: Donald Mitchell Healey, of the Healey Motor Company at Warwick.

HEALEY – THE POST-WAR MIRACLE

Donald Healey had come a long way from his Cornish birthplace. He began designing a sports car during the war, together with Ben Bowden and 'Sammy' Sampietro whom he had met at Humber during war work on armoured vehicles. In 1946, the Donald Healey Motor Company Limited was formally established, and the first Healey Westland Tourer made its sensational debut. This featured a simple but very rigid chassis, an advanced (but expensive) trailing link form of independent front suspension, streamlined bodywork well ahead of most other British cars, and used the well-proven Riley 2½-litre engine which developed nearly 100bhp. The Healey was the fastest British production car

available at the time, with a top speed of 100mph (160kph) – until its crown was stolen by the Jaguar XK120. But the Westland, the Elliot saloon, the Silverstone sports racing car and other Healey models were expensive, and could only be made in penny numbers in the small factory at The Cape, Warwick.

The fledgling Healey company nearly faltered, and would probably have done so had it not been for a generous contract to make the Nash-Healey, a sports model with a Nash engine for this American company to sell in the USA. Even this venture looked like coming to an end in 1952. By then, Donald Healey believed he had spotted an opening in the sports car market, between the MG Midget (the TD series) and the Jaguar XK120. He wanted to develop a relatively inexpensive car, using mass-production components, and with a top speed of 100mph (160kph). He was friendly with Len Lord, and was able to secure an agreement to use Austin's 2.6-litre four-cylinder engine from the ill-fated Atlantic in the new Healey car, together with other assorted Austin parts.

The Sprite was the only Austin-Healey to feature the Austin coat of arms on the badge.

The panel breakline between bonnet and sill remained a Spridget trade mark even after a conventional top-opening bonnet had been introduced in 1961. Pierced wheels were used until 1962 – note the AH letters embossed on the hub cap. The Frog-eye was the only Sprite/Midget model to have identical round front and rear wheelarches.

Donald Mitchell Healey CBE (1898–1988)

Short, a little stocky perhaps, balding from an early age and always with a ready smile, Donald Healey's extrovert personality made him one of the most respected and best-liked figures in the motor industry during his long working life, as well as among the Austin-Healey enthusiasts on both sides of the Atlantic.

He loved his Cornish birthplace and always kept a home at Perranporth, to which he eventually retired. His working life, however, took him much further afield. He was apprenticed to the Sopwith aircraft company at Kingston-on-Thames in 1914, and during World War I flew with the RFC. Demobilized in 1919, he returned to Cornwall and opened a garage business. He took up trials and rallying and, in 1931, won the Monte Carlo Rally in one of the infamous low-chassis Invicta 4½-litre S-types.

In 1933 he moved to Barford, near Warwick, getting his first job in the Midlands motor industry with Riley. He soon moved to Triumph where he became experimental manager and later technical director. He conceived the fabulous Alfa Romeo-inspired Dolomite Straight-Eight of 1934 – sadly to be virtually still-born. He stayed on at Triumph until the original company went bankrupt in 1939. During World War II, he worked on armoured fighting vehicles for Humber.

The birth of the Donald Healey Motor Company and of the first Healey car in 1946 is described in Chapter 1. Several different models of Healey car followed, until Donald hit the jackpot with the Healey Hundred in 1952 – this car very quickly becoming the Austin-Healey 100. Each Austin-Healey car made brought in a royalty payment. The Healey factory at Warwick became an experimental and racing shop, and the original Healey franchise to sell Austin-Healey cars through their own retail premises at Warwick and in London became a general BMC franchise, always with the accent on the sports cars.

Donald got on extremely well with both the difficult Len Lord and with George Harriman (who succeeded Lord as chairman of BMC). In fact the Healey-BMC relationship was amicable through all the years until 1968. It was a blow that the last Big Healey, the 3000, had to be discontinued in 1967, but the unkindest cut of all came when Donald Stokes of BLMC terminated the Healey royalty agreement – and with it, the Austin-Healey name – at the end of 1970. Subsequently, Donald lent his name and expertise to the Jensen–Healey project, but this turned out to be a most frustrating experience. He divested himself of the Healey company at Warwick (by then a Fiat, and later a BMW dealership) but, together with Geoffrey Healey, kept the flag flying as Healey Automobile Consultants at Barford.

Eventually retiring to Cornwall, Donald kept up his active interest in anything to do with the Healey and Austin-Healey cars. He was a much honoured guest at club rallies and events, in the USA as often as in Britain, for as long as his health permitted him to travel. In the closing years of his life, Donald finally wrote his autobiography, part-ghosted by Peter Garnier. It was published posthumously as *My World of Cars* in 1989, with closing chapters by Brian Healey. Although an extremely interesting book, it nevertheless disappointed many readers who had expected Donald to be more frank about some of his contemporaries in the industry. Donald Healey was always the gentleman and remained discreet to the end.

Donald Healey, at the wheel of an Austin-Healey 100 during one of his visits to America.

The 'Big Healey'

The styling of the new car was entrusted to Gerry Coker, who with encouragement and some modifications by Donald developed a remarkably good-looking shape which would happily stand the test of time. Indeed, the bodywork of the 'Big Healey' was very little modified between 1952 and 1968. The resulting car was named the Healey Hundred, and its first tests showed that it was capable of 106mph (170kph), more than justifying the name. The car aroused immense interest when it was introduced in the 1952 Motor Show. Len Lord was so impressed that he struck a deal with Donald Healey – allegedly on the spot, although one suspects there may have been some prior indication of Lord's interest. Whatever the circumstances, the result was that the new car would become the Austin-Healey 100. It would be built in the Austin factory at Longbridge, with Warwick concentrating on design and development work, building specials, together with tuning and race preparation. The first production cars followed in May 1953, and almost 15,000 Austin-Healey 100s were made over the next three years.

This was the birth of what became one of the most legendary British sports car makes. The Austin-Healey name only flourished for a comparatively short period of time, from 1953 to 1970. It was only ever found on a limited number of models, although total production of Austin-Healeys of all types was a respectable 200,000-plus cars. Yet Austin-

AUSTIN-HEALEY '100' WITH HOOD RAISED.

The Austin-Healey 100 was the first car to bear the Austin-Healey name and quickly established itself as a favourite in the sports car market.

Healey is still one of the best-known and most respected British sports cars. In fact, true enthusiasts for the marque would argue that Austin-Healey is second to none – possibly bar MG . . .

MG – A SPORTS CAR HERITAGE

The MG name and pedigree go back to 1923 when a certain Cecil Kimber first launched his MG 14/28 Super Sports model. Kimber was the general manager of Morris Garages in Oxford, from which the famous initials were derived. Not only was this the distributor for Morris cars in Oxfordshire, but it was the original company, owned by William Morris, from which Morris Motors Limited had grown.

Kimber's recipe was quite simple. Take one standard Morris Oxford chassis, tune the engine slightly and clothe it in attractive two- or four-seater sports bodywork, in two-tone colour combinations and with polished wheel discs. Although the MG sports cars quickly developed in more ambitious ways, it was always essential to the Kimber principle to base the cars on such suitable standard components as could be obtained. This was made possible by his company's connections with the large Morris group, which from 1927 onwards also embraced Wolseley.

Production of the original Morris-based MGs went from strength to strength, to the point where Kimber gave up trying to be manager of Morris Garages at the same time and concentrated on MG production – MG cars were now being made in a purpose-built factory on the outskirts of Oxford. It was the new Morris Minor-based MG M-type Midget of 1929, however, which really started the MG success story. Again, it became necessary for Kimber to seek alternative and bigger premises.

He found a part of a leather factory at Abingdon-on-Thames, just over the Berk-

---

The Wolseley Link

The Wolseley link was particularly important. Since 1901, Vickers had owned the Wolseley company, but during the 1920s the business had consistently lost money and, in 1926, Wolseley was declared bankrupt. It was bought by William Morris and remained his personal property until 1935, when he sold it on to Morris Motors Limited. Since 1919, Wolseley had developed a range of overhead camshaft engines, based on a World War I Hispano-Suiza aero engine design which they had made under licence. After the Morris take-over, the Wolseley engineers designed a new small 8hp car with the overhead camshaft engine, destined to become the first Morris Minor. Kimber immediately spotted the possibilities of this engine for use in one of his MG sports cars.

---

shire county border but conveniently close on the south side of Oxford. William Morris agreed to fund the new factory which was opened in early 1930. In the same year, the MG Car Company Limited was formally incorporated, with William Morris as sole owner and Cecil Kimber as managing director.

The Giant Midgets

The M-type was the first of the original Midget line, which would continue unbroken until 1955. With an engine of 847cc, it offered a 65mph (105kph) top speed at a cost of £175. The Midgets grew over the years. The original overhead camshaft engines supplied by Wolseley came to an end in 1936, and were substituted by Morris overhead valve engines in the TA and later models. By 1939, the 1,250cc TB cost £225 and would reach 75mph (120kph). The TD and TF models of the early 1950s were good for about 80mph (130kph), and the final TF 1500 of 1954–1955 would reach 85mph (140kph). With its 1,466cc engine, this last model actually drop-

Introduced at the 1928 London Motor Show, this M-type was the first model to bear the MG Midget name.

ped the Midget name, and its replacement, the MGA, was a fully grown-up sports car which had moved decisively away from the original Midget concept.

Alongside the production models sold to the public, there was an extraordinary diversity of pure racing cars and even record-breakers. These were developed in the period between 1930 and 1935 when William Morris sold the MG company to Morris Motors Limited and the MG racing activities ceased. Many of these racing and record cars had 747cc engines to fit into the international Class H (750cc). In 1931, George Eyston for the first time took a car of this size to over 100mph (160kph), and in the following year, in the famous 'Magic Midget', he reached over 120mph (190kph). When this car was sold to the German driver Bobby Kohlrausch, it achieved even higher speeds. In 1936 near Frankfurt, Kohlrausch drove the 'Magic Midget' at over 140mph (225kph). Development of the racing Midgets went through the C-type, the J.3 and J.4, the Q-type and finally to the R-type of 1935. The R-type was a streamlined single-seater with very advanced independent suspension all round, using torsion bars. It was, however, not fully developed before MG withdrew from racing. In those five years, MG achieved a formidable number of successes in motor sport, and became by far the most popular make of sports car. Indeed, MG and sports car became almost synonymous.

From 1935 onwards, MG was a direct subsidiary of Morris Motors Limited. William Morris was created Lord Nuffield, and gradually the Morris company and its subsidiaries became known as the Nuffield Organization. Cecil Kimber, the man who

Final model of the original MG Midget line was the TF of 1953 to 1955.

With the new 1.5-litre MGA in 1955, MG moved decisively away from the Midget concept.

had founded MG, was sacked in 1941 for having failed to fit in with the master plan for the organization's war-time production. He died in a railway accident in 1945. Fortunately, there were still enthusiasts in charge of the MG factory at Abingdon, and after the war they soon got back to making Midgets. The TC was the first post-war model and was the first MG to make a major impact on overseas markets, including the USA. Its replacement, the TD of 1950, was a runaway success in America, and together with the Jaguar XK120 established a foothold for British sports cars on the other side of the Atlantic. MG's success caused a degree of envy in the Austin company, Nuffield's great rivals, who were as yet without their own

sports car. And then, in 1952, the rivals suddenly became partners.

BMC – THE COMING TOGETHER

Whatever one may say about Leonard Lord, his ambitions for Austin, and his possible desire for revenge on Morris, the idea of merging the two biggest British motorcar manufacturers was a bold and imaginative step. By creating a single corporation of this size, it was hoped that the British motor industry could more effectively meet the growing competition from the American giants (General Motors and Ford with their

---

Leonard Percy Lord (1896–1967, created Lord Lambury 1962)

As a politician, Lord would have been a cartoonist's dream. Big National Health-style spectacles perched precariously on a big nose and bigger ears, bald pate surrounded by wispy strands of hair, prominent teeth and usually to be seen with a cigarette scattering ash everywhere. Born in Coventry, he was described by his great contemporary Miles Thomas as a 'Yorkshire fireball' and was probably of Yorkshire stock, which would explain his blunt personality and distinctly Northern accent!

Always down-to-earth, Lord could sometimes be downright abrasive. His personality – and undoubtedly, his hairstyle – earned him the sobriquet 'Spiky' from the shop-floor. The workforce had probably less to fear from him than his managers or fellow directors. Yet there was a different side to Lord's personality. He was the perfect husband and father, and was capable of kindness as well as selfless generosity.

In 1920, Lord went to work for the Coventry branch of the French Hotchkiss firm. When Morris took over Hotchkiss, Lord came into the Morris sphere of influence, quickly establishing himself as one of the best production managers in the industry. He moved around the Morris empire, spending time re-organizing the Wolseley factory in Birmingham from 1929 to 1932. Then, he was asked to come down to the parent company's main factory at Cowley which badly needed shaking up.

Within two to three years, Lord overhauled Cowley as well as the Morris product range. With the title of vice-chairman, he was the company's number two after William Morris (Lord Nuffield). Feeling entitled to more than just a salaried job, he asked for a share in the business in 1936 but was rebuffed by Nuffield. Following a row, Lord resigned. From this episode dated his wish to beat Morris at their own game, while Lord Nuffield would always think of Lord as the prodigal son.

In 1938 Lord joined Austin at Longbridge. He was clearly being groomed to take over from Lord Austin, as indeed it came to pass. In the post-war period, Lord guided Austin's affairs with a great deal of flair and talent. Not all of his pet ideas were successful, yet by the time of his reconciliation with Lord Nuffield (which led to the BMC merger in 1952), the Austin company was clearly the dominant partner in the marriage.

Lord saw BMC through to 1961, when he stepped down as chairman in favour of the much less ruthless – and much less effective – George Harriman. Becoming honorary president of BMC after Lord Nuffield's death in 1963, Lord himself died a year before his creation, BMC, crumbled under the Leyland onslaught.

European subsidiaries in particular) as well as the big continental manufacturers, especially Volkswagen, Renault and Fiat.

There were numerous problems to overcome before BMC could begin to make sense. Indeed, in some respects, the merger was never fully consummated. For instance, most of the dealer network both at home and abroad remained split in Austin or Nuffield franchises, right through until the BMC-Leyland merger in 1968. What turned out to be another major problem was the multitude of different factory sites, largely a Nuffield legacy, which meant that the corporation was forever transporting components, engines, bodies and even half-finished cars up and down the country. There was also the mutual feeling of rivalry and distrust between the Austin people and the Nuffield people, sometimes egged on by Len Lord himself. One contemporary observer said that merging Austin and Morris was '... like mixing oil with water.'

But on the credit side, there was much in the way of rationalization right from the start. At the time of the merger in 1952, there were eleven different passenger car engines used in BMC cars. At the end of 1956, there were four. Gearboxes and rear axles were similarly rationalized. In 1959, with the advent of the Farina cars, six different body-shells were replaced by two. Badge engineering could never please everybody and the demise of Riley was a direct result of this policy, yet the car buyers at the time seemed happy enough. BMC's output grew steadily from 240,000 cars and light commercials in 1952–1953 to a high point of 730,000 units in 1963–1964.

BMC gave us a wealth of interesting cars, above all, of course, the brilliant Mini. BMC, however, was also always prepared to explore niche-marketing. Sometimes this led to near-disaster – the Vanden Plas Princess 4-litre R springs to mind – sometimes to a fair degree of success, as in the case of the Wolseley 1500 and Riley One-Point-Five. Sometimes, the result was outstanding, as in the case of the Austin-Healey Sprite and MG Midget.

RATIONALIZATION

While BMC never closed any of the many and widespread factories, they opened some new ones, and refurbished several existing plants. Indeed, they could ill afford to lose factory space, trebling as they did car production over a ten-year period. The one area where they did implement rationalization was in the sports car sector. While Austin-Healey cars had initially been assembled in the Austin factory at Longbridge, in the autumn of 1957 production of the 100-Six model was transferred to the MG factory at Abingdon. During a period of a few months, Longbridge and Abingdon both turned out Austin-Healeys, but at the end of the year all cars came from what was henceforth known as BMC's sports car factory. To make way for the Healeys, Abingdon lost final assembly of Riley saloon cars (which went to Cowley and Longbridge) and with the demise of the MG ZA/ZB Magnette at the end of 1958, MG saloon car production was also transferred to Cowley.

Therefore, from the start of Sprite production in 1958, the Sprites were assembled at Abingdon, as were the MG Midgets from 1961 onwards. (The only exception concerned a pilot run of a few hundred cars which were assembled much later in the Morris factory at Cowley.) And, of course, there were the overseas assembly plants, notably in South Africa and Australia, where Sprites and Midgets would be assembled from CKD (Completely Knocked Down) kits sent out from the UK. But in principle, the MG factory at Abingdon became the home of the Sprite and Midget for their combined production run of over twenty-one years, through the BMC and the BL years.

2 Frog-Eye Sprite – Conception and Birth

In the previous chapter, I discussed the background histories of the three makes of car – Austin, Healey and MG – and it is clear that it was MG which pioneered the small, inexpensive sports car for everyman. However, by the mid-1950s MG had largely left this market behind. In response to competition from the Triumph TR2 and the Austin-Healey 100, the MGA of 1955 grew up to become a 1.5-litre sports car, with a top speed of around 100mph (160kph) and a price in the home market of £844 (including tax). At the time, £500–£600 would buy any of the small family cars such as the Austin A30, Ford Anglia/ Prefect or Morris Minor. Meanwhile, the cheapest sports car in regular production was

Without the front bumper, the Frog-eye takes on a different character; it becomes a ready-for-anything, devil-may-care type of car.

The front bumper, technically an option, was fitted to most cars. The wing mirrors are a period accessory. The BMC sticker on the windscreen is a nice touch on such a beautifully restored car.

the Morgan 4/4 at £639. The question now was whether there would be a market for a small sports car at a still lower price?

BARGAIN BASEMENT?

Other people at the time evidently thought so. There was always a ready market for kit cars, such as the original Lotus Seven, and by assembling your own car you saved the Purchase Tax which was as good an incentive as any. Some of the small specialist manufacturers of the late 1950s endeavoured to market small, cheap sports cars. The Berkeley, for example, was really a three-wheeler which had grown an extra appendage. It featured plastic bodywork, a 328cc two-stroke air-cooled two-cylinder engine, and front-wheel drive. It cost £575 in 1957 and would attain 65mph (105kph) on a good day. When Berkeley tried to upgrade their product, with the Ford Anglia-engined Bandit of 1959, they came a cropper. The Turner 950 which used the BMC A-series 948cc engine, cost £550 in kit form or £895 (including tax) in assembled form. A tuned Alexander-Turner reached 95mph (150kph) on road test but cost £1,053 in 1960.

The basic Lotus Seven was not cheap either; in assembled form it cost £1,036 in 1958, but despite its humble side-valve 1,172cc Ford engine still proved good for 80mph (130kph). We may perhaps disregard the Meadows Friskysport (another motorcycle-engined device, like the Berkeley), but this with a rear engine and chain drive was little more than an over-styled bubble car. The early Elvas were literally one-off specials, built for sports car racing, and the 1958 Courier was a 1.5-litre machine using the MGA engine.

Finally, there was the indefatigable Air Vice-Marshall Bennett and his Fairthorpe, rapidly growing up from the rear-engined 250cc Atom of 1954 to the almost-respectable Electron Minor of 1957, with glassfibre body, a 948cc Standard Eight engine and a 75mph (120kph) top speed. Yet the point about all of these was that however well-intentioned or well-designed, they were products of tiny concerns, and even if demand had existed, they would have been completely unable to meet it. Of all these makes, only Lotus and Morgan survive to this day, and neither has been in the sports car bargain basement market for a long time.

It is an error often committed by present-day students of the motor industry to assume that there was such a thing as careful market research in the 1950s. There was not. Most new cars either stuck to well-established market positions or, if they broke new ground, were often the result of inspiration or gut feeling by one or a few individuals. The

Mini is the classic example. Even costing out a new car was not the exact science that Ford later elevated it to with the Cortina in the early 1960s. The idea and concept of the first Sprite seems to have been developed in what, by present-day standards, must be described as a very casual way.

THE A30

Austin had reintroduced a small car for the first time after the war in the 1951 Motor Show, at first calling it the new Austin Seven, but soon adopting the Austin A30 title to fit in with the rest of the range. It was the first Austin car to feature a unitary construction body. It had been cleverly packaged to give room for four passengers and luggage in the smallest possible area, while still using a conventional front-engine/rear-wheel-drive layout. Its suspension – independent at the front with wishbones and coil springs, and with semi-elliptics on the live rear axle – was copybook Austin design, as was the worm-and-peg steering. To save money, the A30 used a peculiar hydro-mechanical braking system: front brakes were fully hydraulic but rear brakes had a mechanical actuation system from a joint hydraulic cylinder under the rear seat.

The most important thing about the A30 was that it was the first car to use what became famous forever after as the BMC A-series engine. The original engine, used from 1951 to 1956, was of 58 × 76.2mm and 803cc. It developed a modest 28bhp at 4,800rpm. The layout of the A-series was derived from the A40 and A70 engines. The crankshaft ran in three main bearings; the camshaft was driven by chain and was mounted low down on the left-hand side. Push-rods and rockers activated the vertical in-line overhead valves. Inlet and exhaust manifolds were both on the left-hand side, fighting for space with the push-rods. All the electrical ancillaries were on the right-hand side of the

BMC A-series engines, as used in the Sprite and Midget from 1961 to 1974.

engine. These early Austin engines had a single Zenith carburettor.

Thanks to its modest dimensions and low weight, the A30 had a fair performance for its day, coupled with excellent fuel economy. It could better the bigger and heavier Morris Minor (fitted with the same engine from 1952 onwards) on both counts. But although it was an endearing little car in many ways, and although it was used for rallying and racing by the intrepid, it did not have the excellent roadholding, handling and steering characteristics of the Morris rival-turned-cousin. Indeed, the rather high and narrow Austin was described by one authority as 'having a penchant for lying over on its door handles'.

THE 'RED DEVIL'

Austin did not have any sporting aspirations with the A30. However, they did make a prototype tourer (which, remarkably, exists to this day) and, in 1953, developed a small sports car, using the A30 mechanical components in a space-frame with a fibreglass body. Dick Burzi, Austin's Argentinian-Italian in-house stylist since 1929, developed proposals in clay model form, and a somewhat different-looking prototype was constructed during the summer of 1953.

The styling had overtones of the Jowett Jupiter, and one remarkable thing about the car was that it had no doors, just rather deep cut-outs to allow entry and exit for driver and passenger. It was totally impossible to do so with the hood in place! The finished prototype was bright red, and was nicknamed 'the red devil'. No one seems to know what happened to it in the end, but the likelihood is that this project was never taken very seriously at Austin, and the car would probably have been far too expensive to build. The bodyshell mouldings were extremely simple but the

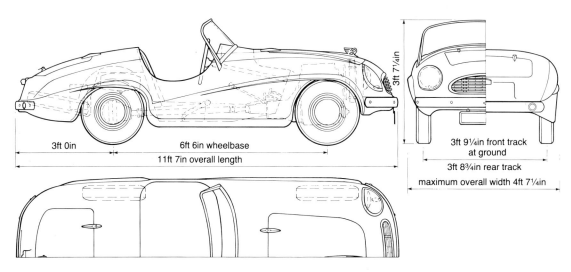

3ft 7¼in

3ft 0in

6ft 6in wheelbase

11ft 7in overall length

3ft 9¼in front track
at ground

3ft 8¾in rear track

maximum overall width 4ft 7¼in

Austin's 1953 proposal for a small plastic-bodied car, based on the A30.

space-frame would have been difficult to manufacture.

It is likely, however, that memories of the red devil remained with Len Lord. (The background story to the Austin-Healey 100 has been covered in Chapter 1.) Once there was regular contact between Lord and Donald Healey, it was natural for Lord to bounce ideas off on the Healeys. Thus, according to Geoffrey Healey's book about the Sprites, *More Healeys*, Len Lord suggested to Donald Healey in 1956 that there was a gap in the sports car market, long since vacated by the Austin Seven Nippy and more recently by MG. Lord said he would like to see a really inexpensive sports car – what he described as a 'bug'.

THE 'BUG'

Donald Healey briefed Geoffrey Healey and the small sports car project became Geoffrey's responsibility. Suitable components were obtained from Longbridge, where in 1956 the 803cc A30 had given way to the 948cc A35, with remote control gearchange and a higher rear-axle ratio. The A35 engine,

gearbox, rear axle and front suspension could all be used in the new car, although the engine was fitted with two SU carburettors to

PBL 75 was a very early Sprite and in its day a much-photographed press car.

Geoffrey Healey (born 1922)

With his large and luxuriant moustache, Geoffrey Healey is guaranteed to stand out in almost any crowd. The oldest of Donald Healey's three sons, he grew up with cars, and it was natural for him to follow in his father's footsteps, serving an engineering apprenticeship and studying at Coventry Technical College.

Geoffrey did his war-time service in the Royal Electrical and Mechanical Engineers. Being de-mobbed from the REME after the war, Geoffrey initially joined the car division of Armstrong Siddeley at Coventry, but seems to have been given more time off than was probably his due, as he often accompanied his father on trips to the USA, or on sporting events. He soon joined the young Healey company at Warwick full time, and helped Donald with the design of the Healey Hundred in 1952. From then on, Geoffrey was closely involved with all of the design and development work carried out at Warwick.

When Donald Healey came back from his meeting with Len Lord in 1956 where the idea for the Sprite had first been mooted, it was Geoffrey that he turned to, and it was Geoffrey who was entrusted with the practical execution of the project. Therefore, the Sprite was really Geoffrey's design. It was also Geoffrey who over the years carried out the continuing development work of the Spridget. It was he also who liaised with Longbridge and Abingdon and who masterminded the Sprite successes at Sebring, Le Mans and in the Targa Florio. In a happy division of responsibility, Geoffrey's two brothers took on separate parts of the Healey business – Brian developing the car sales side at Warwick and in London and John looking after the original Healey family business in Cornwall.

All good things come, sadly, to an end. With the demise of the Austin-Healey in 1970, and the sale by the family of the Donald Healey Motor Company retail business, Donald and Geoffrey became involved with the Jensen Healey project. This led to many complications and much frustration, culminating in 1975 when Jensen had to call in the receiver. With Donald by then having virtually retired to Cornwall, Geoffrey continued to run Healey Automobile Consultants Limited at Barford near Warwick. He became involved in a variety of projects from wind-powered generators via a modified Ford Fiesta to a SAAB-powered sports car. Geoffrey's help and advice were also sought by the Austin Rover Group when it came to testing new cars at nearby Gaydon.

Much more recently, Geoffrey has taken the re-born Healey Frogeye under his wing, and in between has found time to write three interesting books about the Healey company and their cars, modestly withholding much credit for his own contribution to their success.

give the sports model a definitive performance advantage. In this form, the engine developed 43bhp at 5,200rpm (Geoffrey was the oldest of Donald Healey's three sons and he played an extremely important part in the design and development of Healey and Austin-Healey cars.)

There were, however, Austin components which the Healeys deemed unsatisfactory. There proved to be difficulties in getting the A35 steering gear to fit without making the linkage too complicated. Instead, Geoffrey looked elsewhere in BMC's commodious parts bin and came up with the rack-and-pinion steering gear from the Morris Minor. Similarly, the A35's rear-brake linkage did not appeal, so Lockheed was asked to produce

a fully hydraulic set-up. After some calculations, Lockheed came up with smallish-looking 7in drums which worked well enough. The third departure from the A35's mechanical specification concerned the rear suspension. Geoffrey chose quarter-elliptic springs, consisting of fifteen blades and the master leaf. They were anchored in front of the rear axle and worked in conjunction with parallel radius arms above the axle. Three major advantages were cited for this particular layout:

1. There was a reduction in unsprung weight.
2. Axle location was more positive.
3. The suspension stresses were fed directly

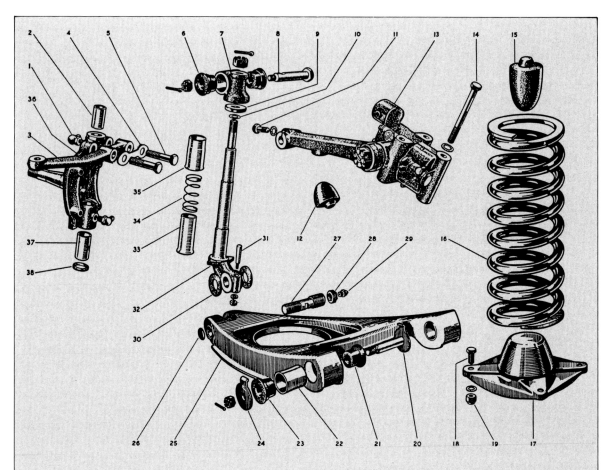

The Spridget front suspension, here as found on the Frog-eye, was very similar to the Austin A35 suspension.

EXPLODED VIEW OF THE FRONT SUSPENSION

1 Lubricator	20 Fulcrum pin
2 Swivel axle bush (top)	21 Rubber bush (bearings)
3 Steering side tube arm	22 Lower link bush (inner)
4 Lockwasher	23 Rubber bush (bearing)
5 Setscrew	24 Special washer
6 Trunnion bush (bearing)	25 Lower link
7 Trunnion link	26 Welch pin
8 Trunnion fulcrum pin	27 Fulcrum pin (outer)
9 Oilite thrust washer	28 Screwed plug
10 Adjustment washer (shim)	29 Lubricator
11 Clamp bolt	30 Cork rings
12 Rebound buffer	31 Cotter
13 Damper	32 Swivel axle pin
14 Setscrews	33 Dust excluder (bottom)
15 Rebound rubber bumper	34 Spring
16 Coil spring	35 Dust excluder (top)
17 Spring seat	36 Swivel axle
18 Bolts	37 Swivel axle bush (bottom)
19 Simmonds nut	38 Cork sealing ring

Austin-Healey Sprite Mark I – Technical Data
Engine type   BMC A-series, four cylinders in line
Bore and stroke   62.9 × 76.2mm
Capacity   948cc
Compression ratio   8.3:1
Valves   In-line overhead valves operated by pushrods
Carburation   Two SU H1 – 1⅛in
Maximum power   43bhp (net) at 5,200rpm
Maximum torque   52lb ft at 3,300rpm
Clutch   Single dry plate, 6¼in (15cm), hydraulically operated
Gearbox   Four-speed manual, synchromesh on 2nd, 3rd and top
Gear ratios   1st 3.627:1, 2nd 2.374:1, 3rd 1.412:1, top 1.00:1, rev. 4.66:1 (optional close ratio box: 1st
    3.2:1, 2nd 1.916:1, 3rd 1.357:1, top 1:1, rev. 4.114:1)
Final drive ratio   4.22:1
Suspension:
    Front: Independent with wishbones and coil springs, lever arm shock absorbers
    Rear: Live axle with quarter-elliptic springs and radius arms, lever arm shock absorbers
Brakes   Drum brakes front and rear, 7in (18cm) drums
Steering   Rack-and-pinion
Wheels   3.5 × 13 ventilated steel disc
Tyres   5.20-13 cross-ply
Wheelbase   80in (2.03m)
Track:
    Front: 45¾in (1.16m)
    Rear: 44¾in (1.14m)
Overall length with front bumper: 139½in (3.54m)
Overall width   53in (1.35m)
Overall height (hood up)   49¾in (1.26m)
Ground clearance   5in (127mm)
Fuel tank capacity   6 Imperial gallons (27 litres)
Weights:
    Kerbside weight: 1,466lb (665kg)
    Gross vehicle weight: 1,816lb (824kg)

PERFORMANCE:
Top speed   83mph (133kph)
0–60mph (0–100kph)   23 seconds
Standing ¼-mile   22 seconds
Fuel consumption   33–40mpg (1,200–1,400km/100l)

into the main load-bearing members of the body structure, which enabled the rear end of the body to be very simple in design.

Students of engineering might care to compare this solution to the cantilever rear suspension of the 1955 Jaguar 2.4-litre, adopted for very similar reasons.

STYLING THE SPRITE

There was no intention ever to give the Sprite anything other than a unitary construction body. This in itself proves that from the start the car was designed with mass production in mind. It may also be pointed out that this was Britain's first open sports car to have a unitary body. All previous sports cars had employed a traditional chassis – arguably

The BMC A-series engine was quite a rational design, with both inlet and exhaust manifolds on the same side, although porting size was restricted, as the pushrods were also on this side of the engine.

All of the electrical ancillaries, plugs, distributor, dynamo and starter motor, were on the other side of the engine. Note the rocker cover label which simply says 'Austin'. The Spridget engines were always green until the early 1970s, but there are several different shades of what is commonly known as 'BMC Engine Green'.

with the exception of the D-type Jaguar, but that at least had a fairly massive front sub-frame! In fact, the Sprite structure could be described as a semi-unitary body. None of the skin panels (barring the sills) were stressed or load-bearing, and the understructure of the car could be described as a chassis. Nevertheless, the whole assembly was welded together, and was designed in steel from the outset – no messing about with fibreglass or aluminium.

The main structure of the car was formed by the floorpan, the sills and the prop-shaft tunnel. The floorpan was braced by a cross-member at the back of the gearbox and, from this, two chassis legs ran forward to support the engine. Stiffness in the scuttle area was added by the footwell boxes, engine bulkhead and inner scuttle structure. At the rear of the floor was a vertical panel leading up to the

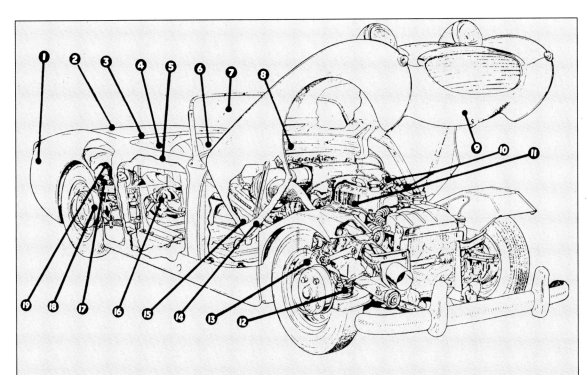

Section drawing of the Healey Frog-eye Sprite, from a BMC press advertisement, May 1958.

1 **Body**, of unitary construction to give tremendous strength without unnecessary weight, is roto-dipped against corrosion. Low total weight (approximately 11 9cwt) gives brilliant performance.
2 **Large luggage compartment** is accessible from inside car.
3 **PVC hood** is easily and quickly assembled. Stows completely out of sight behind seats.
4 **Individual bucket seats.** Driver's seat adjustable. Foam rubber seating upholstered in toughest Vynide.
5 **Trim** includes map pockets in doors.
6 **Steering** is by rack and pinion, 2½ turns from lock to lock. New two-spoke steering-wheel.
7 **Windscreen** is curved, toughened glass. Twin windscreen wipers standard.
8 **Instruments** include oil pressure and petrol gauges, thermometer, ignition warning, headlamp main beam, direction indicator lights. Rev counter is an optional extra.
9 **Easy access front.** Cowl, bonnet and front wing assembly hinge as one unit for complete access to engine and front suspension.
10 **Twin SU carburettors** are fitted for maximum power output.
11 **Engine** is the latest development of the BMC A-series engine which holds several world records. Compression ratio 8.3:1.
12 **Independent front suspension** with coil springs and hydraulic shock absorbers.
13 **Wheels** are fully ventilated for maximum brake cooling. Tubeless tyres.
14 **Gearbox** has four forward speeds. Ratios – first 3.628, second 2.374, third 1.412. Short, remote control gear lever ensures quickest possible gear changes.
15 **Handbrake** is centrally mounted for quick access.
16 **Hypoid rear axle.** Ratio is 4.22:1.
17 **Rear suspension** is by quarter-elliptic springs with trailing links. Independently mounted hydraulic shock absorbers are fitted.
18 **Brakes** are Lockheed hydraulic with 2 leading shoes on front wheels. Total brake area is 67.2 square inches for safe stopping at all speeds.
19 **Fuel tank** holds approximately 6 gallons (27 litres).

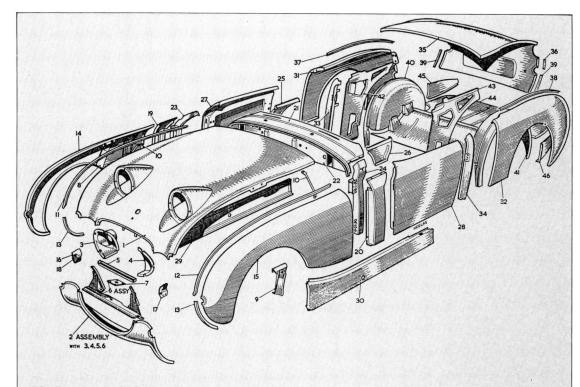

The Frog-eye bodyshell and bonnet assembly.

KEY TO THE BODY SHELL

No.	Description
1	Panel assembly – bonnet top
2	Panel assembly – bonnet front (bottom)
3	Baffle assembly – grille (R/H)
4	Baffle – grille (L/H)
5	Channel – support – grille baffle
6	Reinforcement assembly – bonnet front (bottom)
7	Plate assembly – bonnet lock
8	Bracket assembly – bonnet stay (R/H)
9	Bracket assembly – bonnet stay (L/H)
10	Strut – bonnet
11	Moulding – bonnet top (R/H)
12	Moulding – bonnet top (L/H)
13	Moulding – bonnet – lower
14	Wing assembly – front (R/H)
15	Wing assembly – front (L/H)
16	Bracket assembly – bonnet lock striker (R/H)
17	Bracket assembly – bonnet lock striker (L/H)
18	Bush – striker plate
19	Panel assembly – shroud side (R/H)
20	Panel assembly – shroud side (L/H)
21	Panel assembly – shroud and dash top
22	Panel assembly – dash front top
23	'A' post assembly (R/H)
24	'A' post assembly (L/H)
25	Extension – 'A' post to scuttle (R/H)
26	Extension – 'A' post to scuttle (L/H)
27	Door assembly – less lock (R/H)
28	Door assembly – less lock (L/H)
29	Panel – sill outer (R/H)
30	Panel – sill outer (L/H)
31	Wing assembly – rear (R/H)
32	Wing assembly – rear (L/H)
33	'B' post assembly (R/H)
34	'B' post assembly (L/H)
35	Panel – body rear
36	Moulding – rear wing to panel (intermediate)
37	Moulding – rear wing to panel – top (R/H)
38	Moulding – rear wing to panel – top (L/H)
39	Moulding – lower (rear)
40	Panel assembly – rear wheelarch (R/H)
41	Panel assembly – rear wheelarch (L/H)
42	Reinforcement assembly – 'B' post to wheelarch (R/H)
43	Reinforcement assembly – 'B' post to wheelarch (L/H)
44	Panel assembly – luggage floor
45	Panel assembly – luggage floor to wing (R/H)
46	Panel assembly – luggage floor to wing (L/H)

hump over the rear axle. To this basic assembly were added the front and rear wheelarches, the outer scuttle and door pillars, and the boot floor. Finally came the rear wings and tail panel. To keep the cost down and to keep the structure rigid, there was no bootlid. The front-end assembly, comprising wings and bonnet, was one unit hinged from the scuttle.

The whole understructure could be made with very simple tooling, which helped to keep the cost down. John Thompson Motor Pressings of Wolverhampton, who already made the chassis frame for the bigger Austin-Healeys, took on the job of making the Sprite 'chassis' as well, and were soon able to deliver the first prototypes to Healey's Warwick factory. Gerry Coker, Healey's stylist who had made his name with the original Healey Hundred, also styled the simple body lines of the Sprite.

It had been considered making a car using the same panels for front and rear ends, but this was quickly discarded as being impractical. As ever, the styling was subject to Donald Healey's approval, but because the whole idea was to design a car which would be cheap and simple to manufacture, there was not a great deal of dissent about the way in which the design developed. The body lines that emerged on Coker's drawing board were very simple and functional, but well-proportioned and balanced, and just right from the initial concept. If Coker had any stylistic inspiration it may have been the original Ferrari Barchetta, Pininfarina's 'little boat' from 1949, which also inspired the original AC Ace.

Modifications

There were very few modifications indeed from the first prototype through to production. Because of the low bonnet line falling away to the front, it was difficult to get the headlamps high enough to meet the demands of legislation. Coker originally proposed to

> ### The All-Important Name
> Construction of the first prototype went on during 1956. At this time already, a name was being chosen. Donald Healey selected 'Sprite'. That name had been used on a Riley sports car in the 1930s but had since been registered by the Daimler company for use on a Lanchester model (still-born in 1955). Donald approached the Daimler people and the latter gave their permission for Austin-Healey to take over the name. Thus, when the car was taken to Longbridge for the first time on 31 January 1957, it was already badged as the Austin-Healey Sprite.
>
> John Wheatley, the great Austin-Healey enthusiast who for many years worked as an engineer at Longbridge, remembers being told about the car by a colleague who had seen it arrive at the gate. John was baffled as to what an Austin-Healey Sprite could possibly be!

use pop-up headlamps, arranged in a manner similar to the Porsche 928 twenty years later but, apart from complications with the mechanism when the whole front end of the car had to open up, this proved to be too expensive. Instead, the headlamps ended up in nacelles on the top of the bonnet – the famous feature which was to earn this first Sprite its nickname: the 'Frog-eye' (or, in North America, the 'Bug-eye'). Together with the heart-shaped radiator grille immediately below, these headlamps gave the car a happy, smiling face.

Other slight modifications from prototype to production concerned the door hinges. These, originally external, were replaced by internal hinges, while the line where the sill met the bonnet was modified and tidied up. The facia was somewhat simplified from prototype to production model. The interior was as simple as the exterior. The two bucket seats were upholstered in Vynide, and the floor was covered in rubber mats, coloured to match the trim colour. The facia was also covered in Vynide and only featured the instruments and controls, with a grab handle

The design was kept deliberately simple to reduce manufacturing costs, but despite this – or perhaps because of it – the Frog-eye is an extremely well-balanced and successful car in terms of its styling.

No wind-down windows, only loose sidescreens; so there are roomy pockets behind those simple door trims.

in front of the passenger. There was some stowage space in the doors, however.

The boot and spare wheel had to be reached by tilting the seat backs forward, and then it was a matter of groping around in the dark recesses until you found whatever it was you were looking for. The hood was what was euphemistically described by BMC as the 'pack-away' type – Airfix would have been proud of it – but despite the unpromising appearance of the hood irons and cover, it worked quite well. There were, of course, loose sidescreens, at first of the one-piece type.

THE SPRITE IS APPROVED

Officially, Donald Healey took the car to show to George Harriman (1903–1973). Harriman was then managing director and deputy chairman of BMC, and Len Lord's number two. Lord was abroad at the time, but it seems that Donald first took the car to

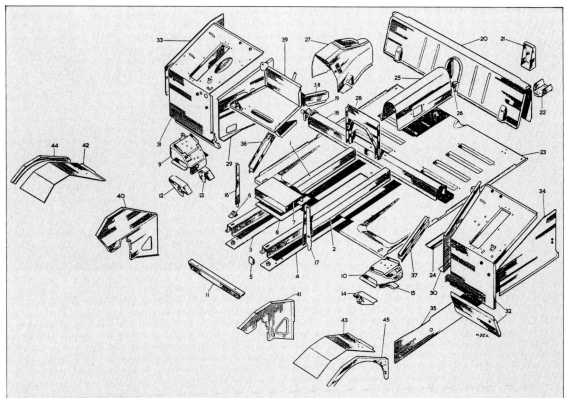

The simple underframe or 'chassis' of the Frog-eye.

KEY TO THE UNDERFRAME

No.	Description
1	Member assembly – frame side (R/H)
2	Member assembly – frame side (L/H)
3	Plate assembly – closing – side member (R/H)
4	Plate assembly – closing – side member (L/H)
5	Plate – end closing – side member
6	Bracket – bonnet locating
7	Cross member – front
8	Plate – closing – front cross member
9	Spring bracket assembly – front syspension (R/H)
10	Spring bracket assembly – front suspension (L/H)
11	Support assembly – suspension housing
12	Bracket – front – front suspension link (R/H)
13	Bracket – rear – front suspension link (R/H)
14	Bracket – front – front suspension link (L/H)
15	Bracket – rear – front suspension link (L/H)
16	Bracket assembly – radiator mounting (R/H)
17	Bracket assembly – radiator mounting (L/H)
18	Cross member assembly – centre
19	Support assembly – jack tube
20	Cross member assembly – rear
21	Bracket assembly – shock absorber mounting (L/H)
22	Plate – spring mounting
23	Floor assembly – main
24	Channel assembly – stiffening – main floor
25	Tunnel assembly
26	Bracket – hand brake abutment
27	Cover assembly – gearbox
28	Panel – tunnel front
29	Panel assembly – inner side – foot well (R/H)
30	Panel assembly – inner side – foot well (L/H)
31	Panel assembly – foot well front and roof (R/H)
32	Panel assembly – foot well front and roof (L/H)
33	Panel assembly – outer – foot well (R/H)
34	Panel assembly – outer – foot well (L/H)
35	Plate – side – sill (L/H)
36	Strut – front suspension (R/H)
37	Strut – front suspension (L/H)
38	Support – heater platform
39	Platform assembly – heater
40	Wheelarch assembly – inner (front R/H)
41	Wheelarch assembly – inner (front L/H)
42	Wheelarch assembly – top (front R/H)
43	Wheelarch assembly – top (front L/H)
44	Wheelarch – outer (front R/H)
45	Wheelarch – outer (front L/H)

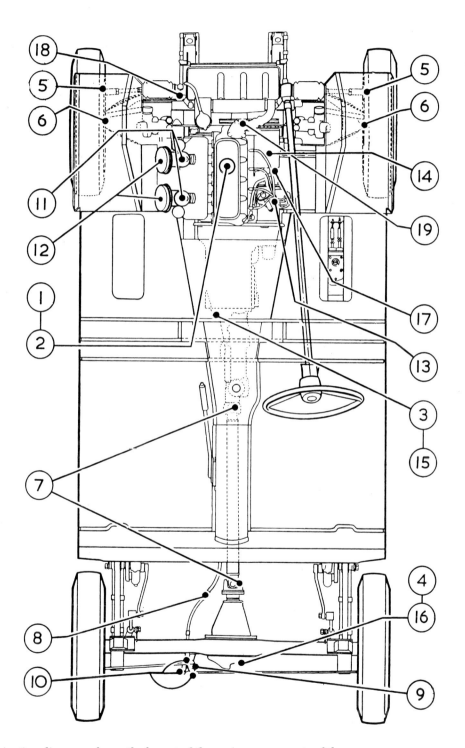

The lubrication diagram shows the layout of the major components of the Frog-eye. Later Spridgets were very similar.

another senior man at Longbridge, Geoffrey Rose, an old friend who was now general manager of the Longbridge factory. Whether he wanted Geoff Rose's opinion on the prospects of making the car at Longbridge, or whether he just wanted a friend's reassurance before going to the top brass is not quite certain! He need not have worried.

Harriman was shown the car in the garage under the Kremlin administration block. Within a few yards was Dick Burzi's styling studio, and not far, Alec Issigonis was busy scheming the Mini. Harriman – who, in contrast to Len Lord, was always the perfect gentleman – liked the Sprite. He told Donald and Geoffrey Healey to bring it back for final approval by Lord when he returned home the following month.

Lord duly saw the car three weeks later, and approved it on the spot. His decisiveness on this occasion matched his reaction when shown the first Healey Hundred in the 1952 Motor Show. Relations between BMC's top men and the Healeys were as amicable as ever. An agreement for the Sprite to be manufactured by BMC, with a royalty payable on each car to Donald Healey, was quickly agreed. BMC now brought in their engineering staff to help making the car ready for production, incorporating the changes mentioned above. The Sprite acquired the official BMC drawing office project number of ADO 13 (lucky for some!), and its official chassis number code of AN5. 'A' stood for small car (capacity less than 1,200cc), 'N' for open two-seater body, and '5' for the series. That number was chosen because the previous Austin-Healey, the 100-Six four-seater, had been the BN4 model (i.e. fourth series) and the current A35 small car range was designated fifth series.

INTRODUCTION AND RECEPTION

Originally, the plans called for the Sprite to

Black was the normal colour for the tonneau cover (as well as for the hood) but both could be supplied in white to special order.

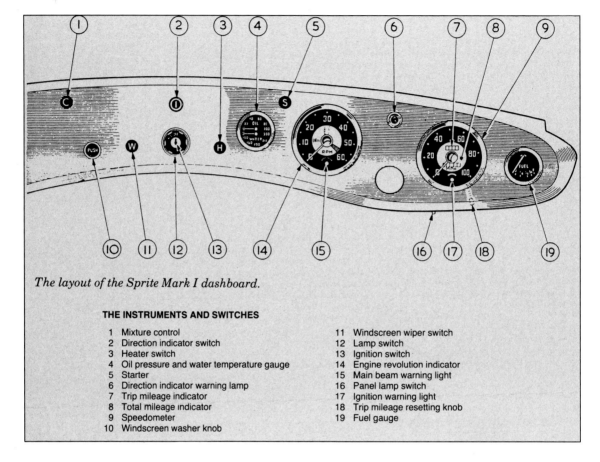

The layout of the Sprite Mark I dashboard.

THE INSTRUMENTS AND SWITCHES

1	Mixture control	11	Windscreen wiper switch
2	Direction indicator switch	12	Lamp switch
3	Heater switch	13	Ignition switch
4	Oil pressure and water temperature gauge	14	Engine revolution indicator
5	Starter	15	Main beam warning light
6	Direction indicator warning lamp	16	Panel lamp switch
7	Trip mileage indicator	17	Ignition warning light
8	Total mileage indicator	18	Trip mileage resetting knob
9	Speedometer	19	Fuel gauge
10	Windscreen washer knob		

be manufactured at Longbridge. However, as we have seen, Austin-Healey production as such was moved to Abingdon in late 1957. Besides, there would have been problems adapting the Sprite design to the existing assembly lines in Longbridge's CAB 1 (Car Assembly Building number 1). So the Sprite ended up joining its bigger brother at Abingdon. John Thompson Motor Pressings supplied the base unit, which was then shipped to Pressed Steel at Swindon, still an independent company (they merged with BMC in 1966), where the remainder of the body panels were added. The finished shell then went to Cowley for painting in the Morris Motors paintshop, and finally to MG at Abingdon, where the cars were assembled, with components coming from many other factories. The engines came down from Morris Motors' engines branch in Coventry, for instance.

Each Sprite therefore went through four different factories, not counting those plants where the mechanical components were sourced. Tortuous indeed. The transportation must have cost BMC a fortune, and whether this was ever taken into account when the products were costed, no one really knows.

A second prototype was constructed in the Healey factory at Warwick, now in close liaison with the BMC engineers from Longbridge and Abingdon. There were one or two little problems to overcome, but production models began to come off the Abingdon production line in March 1958. The chassis num-

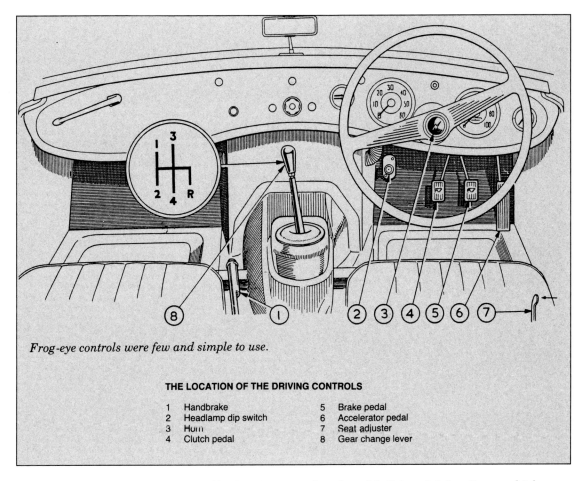

Frog-eye controls were few and simple to use.

THE LOCATION OF THE DRIVING CONTROLS

1	Handbrake		5	Brake pedal
2	Headlamp dip switch		6	Accelerator pedal
3	Horn		7	Seat adjuster
4	Clutch pedal		8	Gear change lever

ber series began with 501 – in Nuffield rather than Austin tradition – and the first car, AN5-L/501, was a left-hand drive model destined for the USA. The public launch was fixed for 20 May 1958, and as this coincided with the Monaco Grand Prix, it was decided to hold the press launch at Monte Carlo.

Press Launch

Donald and Geoffrey Healey both went out. So did BMC sales director Jim Bramley, Austin's publicity manager Reg Bishop and other staff, as well as a large party of journalists, including Tommy Wisdom who was also an accomplished rally driver. BMC shipped out half-a-dozen press cars, both in right-hand and left-hand drive form, which were registered by the local Austin agents under the French equivalent of trade plates. The Healeys also took their own Sprite, YAC 740, with a tuned engine, for Donald and Tommy Wisdom to take over the course of the Italian Mille Miglia road race.

Apart from Tommy Wisdom being photographed in the act of painting graffiti on a wall somewhere in Italy – 'Viva Healey', naturally – all went well. The reception both from Fleet Street and from the motoring magazines was all that the Healeys, and

(Overleaf) No wonder the Frog-eye has the capability of inspiring affection.

The underbonnet layout of the Frog-eye was a little more cluttered when the optional heater was fitted. On this car, the bonnet opens the wrong way.

BMC, could have wanted. The headline in *The Motor* proclaimed that 'Entirely New Sprite Model ... Brings Sports-car Motoring Back to Economy Class'. In an advertisement in *Motor Sport* for May 1958, BMC blew their own trumpet under the banner of 'Hail to thee, blithe Sprite' – which did not, however, catch on as a general sales slogan. In the June issue of the same journal, Bill Boddy spoke of the 'happily-smiling Sprite'. *The Autocar* confidently predicted that '...there is certainly a large market awaiting it'. *The Autocar* also referred to pre-launch rumours and stated that 'most of these legends sug-

gested a new MG'. Most contemporary writers, however, took their cue from the Austin company's press release and mentioned the Austin Seven Nippy somewhere, especially when they compared the Sprite's quarter-elliptic rear suspension to the similar arrangement found on its forebear.

The praise heaped on the new car by most newspapers was even more lavish, although the *Manchester Guardian* (as it was in those days) struck a sour note by declaring that the headlamps '... appear to have been added as an after-thought and sit rather uncomfortably on the bonnet'. Spoilsports ...

Nothing new in celebrity races ... Jack Brabham and Stirling Moss were among the drivers taking part in an Austin-Healey Sprite race, held before the British Grand Prix at Aintree in 1959.

Two intrepid Scotsmen, Andrew Henderson and David Philp, took their Frog-eye round the world in 1959–1960, but stopped to have their picture taken at BMC's headquarters at Longbridge.

The well-rounded rump has a pert, almost provocative look.

Proper road tests soon appeared in the specialized journals, and even after more extensive testing, there were few faults or shortcomings to be pointed out. The same road test car (PBL 75) went to both *The Motor* and *The Autocar* in that order. Perhaps for this reason, *The Motor* measured a top speed of 83mph (133kph) whereas *The Autocar* could not get it over 81mph (130kph). Also, *The Autocar* reported that the exhaust system broke away from the manifold while on test ... Both magazines agreed that the worst feature on the car was the access to the boot, or rather lack of it. But at a total price of

£669, including Purchase Tax, there was a universal welcome for the Sprite as a return to the pre-war ideal of a low-cost, economical sports car for the less wealthy enthusiast.

THE FROG-EYE GOES ABROAD

Sprites were shipped out to the USA and Canada right from the start of production. The suggested list price was $1,795 in New York (around £640 at the then prevailing rate of exchange; the list price before tax in the UK was £445). *Road & Track* tested the Sprite in August 1958, and did they get it wrong! They referred to it as the 'long-awaited Morris Minor (sports) version', and they were not at all clear why the car was called the Austin-Healey Sprite ('the car wasn't designed and will not be built by Donald Healey'). They did not like the looks of the car but conceded that 'appearance notwithstanding, the Sprite has some very attractive features...' They managed a top speed of 80mph (130kph), and concluded in a positive vein: 'It offers more fun per dollar than anything we have driven for a long time.'

There were excellent reports in motoring magazines in Australia, Canada and many other countries. The Swiss *Automobil Revue*, highly respected for accuracy and impartiality, summed up the Sprite as 'uncomplicated fun' (*'einfach und munter'*), where the German word *munter* also suggests optimism and liveliness. Their French-language edition used the word *fringante* which means high-spirited, possibly bordering on the cheeky! Well, it was that sort of car...

3 The Frog-Eye in Production

The Sprite Mark I was actually in production for less than three years. There were remarkably few modifications done to the car during this period, as the list found later in this chapter will testify. Most of these modifications occurred relatively early in the production run, probably in swift response to teething toubles, from which, however, the Sprite seems to have been remarkably free. The small number of modifications might be cited in evidence of the basic soundness of the design.

Of the three niggling little problems that initially affected the car, two were successfully remedied within a year: firstly, the seal between the windscreen frame and the hood was improved, and secondly, the ignition coil was moved from the dynamo where it had suffered from engine vibration. Only the frail rev counter drive box which was located on the end of the dynamo remained as a source of irritation to owners, especially in cold climates, where it tended to break every winter.

One of the reasons why the Sprite could be sold at the relatively low price of £445 basic, or £668.17.0 including Purchase Tax ($1,795 in the USA) was that the car was not at all well-equipped in standard form, and very few cars were made without some extra equipment being fitted. The following is a list of those optional extras which were offered when the model was first introduced, with prices including Purchase Tax (with no apologies for quoting these prices in old-fashioned money – remember pounds, shillings and pence?):

Heater and demister	£20.16.3
Rev counter (tachometer)	£4.10.0
Front bumper with overriders	£6.0.0
Windscreen washer	£2.5.0
Laminated windscreen glass	£4.2.6
Locking petrol filler cap	18.9
Tonneau cover	£6.0.0
Dunlop Fort six-ply tyres	£7.2.6
Fresh-air unit (alternative to heater)	£6.0.0
Radio	£25.0.0

Since the first four items (heater, rev counter, front bumper and windscreen washer) were fitted to the vast majority of cars, the actual cost of most Sprites would therefore be £702.8.3 including Purchase Tax, while on export models destined for the important North American market, these four items were fitted as standard, together with the laminated windscreen. Standard home market cars had toughened windscreen glass.

Further options and extras which became available during the production run included hood, sidescreens and tonneau cover in white rather than black. A fibreglass hard-top became available, usually in white, sometimes in black. Healeys at Warwick offered their own alternative hard-top, made for them by Jensen at West Bromwich. If a hard-top was fitted from the factory, it was supplied with much improved sliding sidescreens with aluminium frames, and these were eventually standardized on all cars in 1960. Other extras which became available included twin wind-tone horns, a cigar lighter, a luggage rack and a wing mirror.

This Frog-eye sports the optional hard-top, together with the later sliding sidescreens.

SPRITELIER STILL

Those options and extras discussed so far were those which could be specified when a new car was ordered. In a different category altogether, and most certainly not available factory-fitted on new cars, were a whole range of engine tuning and competition parts, available either from BMC or from Donald Healey Motors at Warwick. Among the special parts offered by BMC to make the Sprite go that bit quicker were the following:

- Flat-top pistons, for a 9.3:1 compression ratio

- Special competition camshaft
- Stronger valve springs with special collars
- Competition-type crankshaft
- Heavy-duty exhaust valves
- Lightened flywheel and competition clutch
- Distributor with modified advance curve
- Thermostat outlet blanking sleeve
- Set of close ratio gears (top 1:1, 3rd 1.357:1, 2nd 1.916:1, 1st 3.2:1, rev 4.114:1)
- Alternative rear axle ratios (5.735:1, 4.875:1, 4.555:1, 3.900:1, 3.727:1)
- Speedometer heads to suit above-mentioned ratios

Old English White was always a popular colour, offered with a choice of either red interior trim, as seen on this Frog-eye, or black.

- Specially tuned exhaust system including exhaust manifold
- Competition front shock absorbers
- Adjustable rear shock absorbers
- Strengthened road wheel (standard on later Sprite Mark II models)

The still more ambitious owner could apply to Healeys at Warwick who were prepared to supply the following items:

- Pair of 1¼in carburettors, with special inlet manifold and cold air box

Mark I, 948cc (G-AN1), from introduction (1961) to October 1962

Exterior	Trim	Hood	Hard-top (if fitted)
Old English White	Black	Grey	Dark Grey or Old English White
Old English White	Red	Grey	Dark Grey or Old English White
Tartan Red	Black	Red	Tartan Red or Old English White
Tartan Red	Red	Red	Tartan Red or Old English White
Black	Red	Grey	Dark Grey or Old English White
Clipper Blue*	Dark Blue	Dark Blue	Dark Blue or Old English White
Farina Grey*	Red	Grey	Dark Grey or Old English White

*These two colours may have been found only on the early cars, and may have been replaced as early as September 1961 by the following colours:

Exterior	Trim	Hood	Hard-top (if fitted)
Ice Blue	Blue	Dark Blue	Dark Blue or Old English White
Dove Grey	Red	Grey	Dark Grey or Old English White

Mark I, 1,098cc (G-AN2), from October 1962 to January 1964

Exterior	Trim	Hood	Hard-top (if fitted)
Old English White	Black	Black	Old English White
Old English White	Red	Grey	Old English White
Old English White	Hazelnut	Hazelnut	Old English White
Tartan Red	Black	Red	Tartan Red or Old English White
Tartan Red	Black	Black	Tartan Red or Old English White
Tartan Red	Red	Red	Tartan Red or Old English White
Black	Red	Black	Dark Grey or Old English White
Black	Hazelnut	Hazelnut	Dark Grey or Old English White
Ice Blue	Blue	Dark Blue	Dark Blue or Old English White
Dove Grey	Red	Grey	Dark Grey or Old English White
British Racing Green	Black	Black*	Old English White
British Racing Green	Hazelnut**	Hazelnut**	Old English White

*A few green cars with black trim had grey hoods.
**Hazelnut trim and hood were rare on green cars.

- Polished cylinder head
- Polished connecting rods
- Oil cooler kit
- Dual exhaust system
- Dual exhaust system, with Servais silencer and chrome-plated tail pipes
- Wire wheel and front disc-brake conversion kit
- 8in front drum brake conversion kit
- Anti-roll bar kit
- Stiffer shock absorber valves, front and rear
- Stiffer front and rear springs
- Quick-action filler cap

It is quite important to point out that *no* Sprite Mark I ever had either wire wheels, or front disc brakes, as it came off the Abingdon production line. Those works racing cars (especially those prepared for Sebring) which were so equipped were modified by Donald Healey at Warwick. All other cars which may now be equipped with wire wheels or disc brakes are modifications carried out for or by private owners, at the time or in later years.

SPECIAL TUNING

BMC, as was their practice, issued a Special Tuning booklet for the Sprite, bearing the usual dire warning that 'Power Costs

Without the front bumper the Frog-eye looks even cheekier but rather naked.

Money', and then describing five different tuning conditions which would increase the power output of the Sprite.

The first step was to polish the ports and combustion chambers, which should result in an extra 2bhp. As a second stage, it was recommended to fit the flat-top high compression pistons in addition to stage one, and re-set the ignition timing to 3deg BTDC, for a total of 47bhp. The third tuning condition was based on the first two, but also called for fitting the stronger valve springs, the competition camshaft, special distributor and alternative carburettor needles. With ignition set at 1deg BTDC and using premium fuel, output should be 50bhp at 5,800rpm. The fourth tuning condition incorporated all previous tuning conditions and, in addition, prescribed widened inlet and exhaust ports, which should produce a further 2bhp. Finally, the fifth tuning condition called for fitting the special exhaust system in conjunction with any of the previous four stages, which would yield another 2–3bhp.

All of these modifications were fairly modest and there were and are other more drastic modifications which can be made to the long-suffering A-series engine by those who seek the ultimate in performance from a Sprite or Midget!

The Frog-eye never had a rear bumper, only these overriders to protect its well-rounded rump.

SPECIAL AND MODIFIED FROG-EYES

No sooner, it seems, had the Sprite made its official debut than the improvers got busy on it. One of the first in the field was John Sprinzel of Speedwell (*see* Chapter 10) whose first Speedwell Sprite was made available for press demonstrations in the summer of 1958. This particular car was none other than PMO 200, an early works Sprite that Sprinzel had persuaded the Competitions Department at Abingdon to part with, and which later became one of the most famous Sprite registra-tion marks after its numerous rally appearances.

In its original Sprinzel-improved form, the Speedwell Sprite featured larger 1½in carburettors, a polished cylinder head and a raised compression ratio of 8.7:1. This resulted in more than 50bhp, and Speedwell offered to convert Sprites to this stage of tuning for £72.10.0. The car was also fitted with Speedwell's anti-roll bar. Press reports mentioned that Speedwell was developing a fibreglass bonnet, a hard-top and a wire-wheel conversion kit for the Sprite. There was also a 60bhp 'second stage' tuned version

*Open wide ... You can see almost everything under the Frog-eye
bonnet, but it is not easy to get access to the battery right at the back.*

on the way, and PMO 200 was modified to
this level before being entered in the Alpine
Rally in July 1958. The 'first stage' Speedwell
Sprite was already good for almost 90mph
(145kph).

PMO 200 soon acquired one of the early
Speedwell-type bonnets, looking somewhat
like the original Lotus Elite. Like most alternative Frog-eye bonnets, it was hinged at the
front. In August 1958, PMO 200 ran in the
Liège-Rome-Liège with this bonnet, but still

on disc wheels and with the original type
Speedwell hard-top, which featured a pronounced wrap-around rear window. Later
Speedwell bonnets sometimes featured
swage lines running aft from the front
wheelarches, and headlamps set behind
Perspex fairings.

Eventually Sprinzel – by then no longer
associated with Speedwell – developed a different bonnet, with the standard Frog-eye
grille, and wing-mounted headlamps like the

The black and silver instrument dials were an Austin-Healey feature. The dashboard was always covered in vynide to match the interior trim, but the floor should be covered in a red rubber mat.

By unscrewing the stanchions from the scuttle on each side of the car, the whole windscreen frame is easily removed, and aeroscreens can be fitted for racing.

later Sprite Mark II. This bonnet was found on a later incarnation of PMO 200, with a much prettier special hard-top which had a specially shaped windscreen and sidescreens. In this form, PMO 200 had wire wheels, and was seen in a number of rallies, including the 1960 RAC. It was also seen on the race tracks, where the high point of its career was the 1961 Sebring race.

John Sprinzel had by then built so many of these modified Sprites that his car could be officially homologated as a GT car, and he even issued a sales brochure. After the 1961 Sebring race, he adopted the name 'Sebring Sprite' for his cars. This has ever since led to some confusion over what exactly is a real Sebring Sprite, and which of these were the actual works cars?

SEBRING SPRITES

Sprinzel offered his Sebring Sprites in six different stages of tune, of which the most hairy was a supercharged 87bhp engine costing £290.0.0. The actual specification of his cars could be totally tailored to customer demands.

By 1961, the Sprinzel Sebring Sprite was an impressive little beast, featuring a BMC Formula Junior crankshaft, flat-top pistons with an 11:1 compression ratio, and 1½in

On this racing Sprite, the special bonnet gives the car an almost Ferrari-like look.

Modifications to the Sprite Mark I 1958–1961

Engine number 9C-U-H/1073 New type of thermostat.
Engine number 9C-U-H/1397 Valves modified.
Engine number 9C-U-H/1551 New type of carburettor float chamber lids.
Gearbox number 946 Improved synchromesh on 3rd/4th gears.

The following modifications are all by car/chassis number:

AN5/1606 Modified door-top finishers, sidescreen mounting brackets and sidescreens.
AN5/3444 Improved rev counter cable (RHD cars only).
AN5-L/3689 Improved speedometer cable (LHD cars only).
AN5/4333 Rear axle casing with modified shock absorber mounting points.
Luggage rack offered as optional extra.
AN5/4695 New air-intake behind radiator grille.
AN5/4800 Steering lever with single bolt instead of two-bolt fixing.
AN5/5477 New windscreen frame with improved hood fixing for better waterproofing.
Hard-top offered as optional extra.
AN5/6433 Modified swivel axle assembly and front hub bearing.
AN5/6892 Horns mounted on separate brackets.
AN5/6901 Windtone horns offered as optional extra.
AN5/10344 New type of interior door handles.
AN5/11889 Ignition coil moved from dynamo to inner wing valance.
AN5/13545 White hood, sidescreens and tonneau cover offered as alternative to black.
AN5/26724 Tudor twin-jet windscreen washer of improved type.
AN5/36194 Number-plate lamp with two bulbs.
AN5/41016 Flexible section added to fuel line just before petrol pump.

(At some time during 1960, the aluminium-framed sliding sidescreens, originally offered in conjunction only with the hard-top, were standardized on all cars.)

---

carburettors. The later cars used the close-ratio gearbox from the Sprite Mark II, typically with a 4.55:1 final drive. An anti-roll bar, wire wheels, front disc brakes, heavy-duty front shock absorbers and adjustable rear shock absorbers were all part of the package. With a fibreglass bonnet, an aluminium hard-top and almost bereft of interior trim, weight was under 12cwt (610kg). This proved one of the few Frog-eye derivatives capable of a genuine 100mph (160kph), but at a price: the equipment fitted to such a car totalled almost £650 which doubled the cost of a new Sprite.

The Sprinzel-developed cars were not the first Sebring Sprites, however. The Donald Healey Motor Company Limited at Warwick had prepared a team of four special Sprites for the 1959 Sebring race. These had 57bhp engines, hard-tops, wire wheels and front disc brakes. Geoffrey Healey claimed a top speed of 98mph (158kph) for these cars, but when *Road & Track* tested such a car in 1960 – whether a genuine 1959 race car, or a replica, was not specified – they measured a top speed of 88mph (141.5kph), still a worthwhile improvement from standard. *Road & Track* pointed out that it was perfectly possible to create a replica Sebring Sprite, all of the necessary parts being available from BMC or Healey, as described earlier in this chapter. In the USA, BMC importers Hambro also sold the Healey-sourced parts.

Subsequent developments of the works racing Sprites were not made generally available to the public, but Healey did offer a variety of tuning packages. They listed a conversion set incorporating wire wheels and Girling disc brakes for £89, and would also convert a car to wire wheels retaining the

The headlamp nacelles are separate pressings.

existing drum brakes. A Warwick-tuned Sprite with a 'fourth stage' engine recorded almost 92mph (148kph) in the hands of *The Motor* in April 1959. The car was also fitted with the close-ratio gears and 1¼in carburet-

The Frog-eye rear wheelarch – the round arch which was only to return for a brief period on the MG Midget in the early 1970s.

tors, neither of which were available any more by then (!). The total cost of modifications was just over £166, including wire wheels and disc brakes, but excluding the gearbox, carburettors and the hard-top fitted to the test car.

SUPERCHARGER ET AL

In many ways, it was a simpler solution to fit a supercharger to the Sprite. Healeys became sole distributors for the Shorrock kit in 1960. This could be fitted to any car with the BMC A-series engine, and cost £82 including fitting. The Shorrock vane-type supercharger was driven by V-belts from a special crankshaft pulley, and there was a single 1½in SU carburettor on a special manifold. The result was 68bhp at 5,700rpm, and a top speed of over 90mph (145kph). It was recommended to fit harder Champion N3 plugs instead of the standard N5 type, also a steel-asbestos cylinder head gasket. Apart from the fairly modest cost, the attraction of the supercharger was that it was easy to install or remove, and gave a considerable increase in performance.

Other tuning wizards waved their magic wands over the Frog-eye. A Downton-tuned car was built for sports car racing in 1959. It had an improved cylinder head with larger valves, a high-lift camshaft, 1¼in carburettors, a compression ratio of 10.3:1 and a lightened flywheel. The cost of this conversion was approximately £100 including fitting, and the top speed was just over 90mph (145kph).

Paddy Gaston, one of Downton's drivers, later developed his own Sprite GT which was displayed in the 1961 racing car show. The engine was bored out to 994cc and had all the usual tuning modifications, and the car was capable of just about 100mph (160kph). It was fitted with a special bonnet and hard-top by Ashley Laminates, and as it was intended

It can be a bit of a squeeze getting in and out of a Frog-eye or indeed any Spridget, the doors are narrow and the deep sills are necessary for the structural integrity of the car.

as a road-going GT car, also had improved seats, full carpeting and a wood-rim steering-wheel. Other Gaston-inspired touches included a ZF differential, and another wire-wheel-cum-disc-brake conversion. You needed a fairly deep pocket, however, to buy a replica, which would have cost close to £1,000.

The Alexander-tuned Sprite would reach 100mph (160kph), if fitted with an aero screen and a half-tonneau cover – in normal road-going trim top speed was more likely to be 92mph (148kph). There was nothing extraordinary about the engine tuning, but an interesting feature was the vacuum brake servo. The Alexander car kept the drum brakes and disc wheels, but sported some fancy wheel trims and was shown off to the press with a strange contrast-colour flash down the sides.

The rear lights were also found on the Morris Minor 1000 and countless other vehicles, while also the indicators and number-plate lamp were standard Lucas items.

COMFORT, CONVENIENCE OR COSMETICS

There were other options available for those who were less concerned with making the Sprite go faster. Those who were oblivious to the charm of that happy, froggy-eyed face could pick from a number of alternative bonnets. These were mostly made from fibreglass which helped to reduce weight, and some (such as the Speedwell bonnet) also had better aerodynamic properties. The bonnets were usually hinged at the front, which gave better access to the engine compartment and the often overlooked battery.

The most successful non-standard bonnets kept the Sprite grille and so had a family resemblance. They included the first of them all, made by Peasmarsh Reinforced Plastics, as well as the Ashley bonnet and the later Sprinzel bonnet. A particularly good-looking version was made by the Swiss Austin importer, Emil Frey of Zürich.

The Speedwell bonnet was the finest of those that used non-standard grilles. In the USA, Dama Plastics of Pennsylvania modelled their design on the Lancia and Ferrari racing cars, while J Geddes of California offered a bonnet with a very ordinary American-style full-width grille. Some erstwhile Frog-eyes ended up in later years as Jaguar E-type look-alikes, but are usually betrayed by their less generous proportions and a certain lack of finesse in the execution!

A number of different hard-tops were available for the comfort lovers, in addition to the standard factory item. The Jensen-made hard-top offered by Healeys at Warwick had external clips fitting to the windscreen frame and required its own type of sliding sidescreen. The original Speedwell hard-top with the panoramic rear window has been mentioned, as have the later Sprinzel aluminium hard-tops. A Sprite fitted with a Sprinzel hard-top and bonnet was a pretty little car, in the manner of the Lotus Elite. The Ashley Laminates hard-top had a bul-bous fastback style which promised plenty of headroom and also gave some extra stowage space inside. It could be used with the standard sidescreens, which was an advantage. Well made it was, but pretty it was not ...

Finally, mention should be made of the BMC range of approved accessories, which were not factory-fitted but were sold in the aftermarket by BMC dealers. Many of these were tools or loose items, or were common to several cars in the BMC range, like wheel rimbellishers or wing mirrors. Items peculiar to the Sprite included fitted seat covers in a variety of patterns, and a child's seat in various colours to match Sprite interior trim. This fitted over the transmission tunnel between the seats and would not meet with the approval of safety campaigners a generation later! You could also fit your Sprite with an electric clock, a reversing lamp and even an ashtray (with Austin motif), courtesy of BMC.

THE SPRITE ABROAD

Most markets were supplied with fully-assembled Sprites direct from Abingdon, and in the pre-1968 period there was little in the way of difference between Sprites for different export markets. In fact, left-hand drive, a kilometres' speedometer, and various types of headlamp were the most important export variations. But for some markets, Sprites were supplied in the form of Completely Knocked Down (CKD) kits. CKD means that the cars are exported unassembled, in large crates full of bits and pieces and this is done to get around import restrictions or customs barriers in the receiving countries. Such kits may be more or less complete, depending on legislation requiring local content, made in the country of assembly. The CKD Sprites were typically not only unassembled but unpainted, and items such as electrical parts, glass, tyres and some trim parts were often of local manufacture.

The Innocenti Story

Two brothers Innocenti founded a company in Milan in 1933, making press tools for the rapidly-growing Italian motor industry. With the outlook uncertain in the immediate post-war period, they looked around for another product, and hit upon the idea of making a cheap motorcycle which would be suitable as everyday transport for the Italian common man – and woman. Looking as if it might have been inspired by the war-time British Corgi, designed to be dropped by parachute, the first Innocenti-made Lambretta scooter of 1947 featured small wheels and an engine hidden away under the saddle. It was largely made up of steel pressings, which included running boards, a front apron, and fairings for the front wheel.

Not quite as adventurous as the contemporary Vespa (another Italian product), the Lambretta built up a sizeable following over the years, and made an enormous contribution to putting war-torn Italy back on wheels. However, there is a tide in the affairs of scooter manufacturers. The new Fiat 500 car of 1957 was a serious blow to Lambretta and Vespa – a car so cheap that it was possible for many scooter owners to afford it.

Both the scooter manufacturers hedged their bets. Vespa developed its own small car, subsequently produced over the border in France, and the Innocenti people negotiated an agreement with the British Motor Corporation to assemble selected BMC cars in Italy. The start was made with the Austin A40 (appropriately an Italian design) which was launched in the 1960 Turin Motor Show. The complete mechanical kits were supplied from Britain but, using their long-standing expertise, Innocenti made their own body panels.

The other Innocenti model was the Spyder. This used the Sprite's mechanical components and, this time, sported a Ghia-designed body built by OSI on Innocenti presses. Further BMC-based models were to follow. The Innocenti IM3 was a de-luxe version of the 1962 Morris 1100, and a cheaper J4 followed. Most enduringly popular were the Innocenti versions of the Mini, which included the basic saloon, the automatic saloon, the Traveller and the Mini-Cooper which was kept in production in Italy for much longer than in Britain.

In the late 1960s, Innocenti attempted to revive flagging scooter sales by introducing a new Bertone-designed Lambretta, but this failed in the competition against Japanese motorcycle makers. Perhaps as a result of this, Innocenti was taken over by British Leyland in 1972. Geoffrey Robinson (later to become managing director of Jaguar, and then a Labour MP for Coventry) was put in charge. During his tenure, Innocenti introduced the Regent – an attempt at making the Allegro speak Italian.

However, the Italians gave the Regent the cold shoulder, and with British Leyland's growing problems in Britain (which led to its virtual nationalization in 1975), the Innocenti subsidiary was deemed superfluous to requirement.

In any case, after Britain's entry into the Common Market in 1973, the Continental markets could equally as easily be supplied from British factories. So in 1976, Innocenti was sold to the Argentinian Alejandro de Tomaso who was building his own empire of specialist motorcycle and car manufacturers.

The only Innocenti model which continued in production was the Bertone-styled 'New Mini' of 1974, the car that some people thought was going to replace the Mini also in Britain. Later versions of this car abandoned the BMC A-series engine in favour of a Japanese Daihatsu three-cylinder engine. De Tomaso eventually sold Innocenti to Fiat, who at the moment seem to be keeping Innocenti in limbo. They do, however, have the intention to use the Innocenti dealer network for selling certain of the East European Fiat-based products in Italy.

Originally, CKD Sprites were supplied to Eire and to South Africa, and a few batches of left-hand drive cars were sent to Mexico in this form. A considerable boost to CKD production came in 1959, when Sprites in kit form began to be exported to Australia. The cars, assembled by the Pressed Metal Corporation at Enfield, near Sydney in New South Wales, came on the market in 1960. The Australian-assembled Sprites had their own unique colour range of Nürburg White, Monza Red, Le Mans Blue and Goodwood Green. Thanks to the locally-assembled cars, Australia became one of the best export markets for the Sprite, outside North America.

THE ITALIAN CONNECTION

In 1960, BMC began to send partial CKD kits to Italy. These kits consisted only of the mechanical parts but contained no body or trim parts, and they were supplied to the Innocenti company in Milan. Innocenti had conceived the Innocenti 950 Spyder, incorporating Sprite mechanical parts in a Ghia-designed body, made by OSI on Innocenti presses. The Innocenti was not unlike the later Sprite Mark II in looks but was perhaps rather neater. Additionally, it boasted worthwhile amenities compared to the Frog-eye, such as an external boot-lid, a glove-box and wind-up windows.

There was a price to be paid for the additional comforts of the Innocenti. The weight was up from the 13cwt (650kg) of the Frog-eye to some 14cwt (700kg). Then, the car cost appreciably more in those countries where the Innocenti sold against the Spridget (often marketed by the same importer). In 1961, the Frog-eye cost 7,800S.fr. in Switzerland, but the Innocenti was 10,250S.fr. In 1964, the Innocenti was introduced in the USA where it cost $2,920, over $800 more than the standard car.

On performance, the Innocenti 950 Spyder compared well with the standard car. *Road & Track* tested a Sprite in 1963 and an Innocenti in the following year. Both were fitted with 1,098cc engines, and produced similar top speeds and acceleration times. The Innocenti was perhaps slightly heavier on fuel.

The original 950 Spyder was progressively updated along with the Spridget. In 1961–1962, the Innocenti kits were based on the Sprite Mark II (H-AN6 model), and in 1963 the Italian car became the Innocenti S fitted with the 1,098cc engine from the H-AN7 Sprite model. Until 1964, the Innocenti-destined kits were still issued with regular Sprite chassis numbers (although they were not counted as part of the normal Abingdon production). When the Sprite went to the Mark III model in 1964, however, Innocenti began to issue their own serial numbers.

Also in 1964, the Innocenti adopted front disc brakes and semi-elliptic rear springs in tandem with the Spridget, but the Innocenti never received the 1,275cc engine fitted to the Spridget in 1966. The smaller engine was more advantageous under Italian tax regulations, and from then on the twin-carburettor 1,098cc engine was made by BMC specially for Innocenti.

On the other hand, the Innocenti was face-lifted by OSI in 1967, emerging with a new radiator grille and side lamps and, more importantly, with a fixed coupe roof. In this form, the car was known as the Innocenti C Coupe, and continued in production until 1970. Based on the known serial numbers, production of the Innocenti Spyder amounted to 7,668 cars between 1960 and 1964, and it is probable that the total number made until 1970 was between 15,000 and 20,000 cars, most of which were sold in the Italian home market.

4 Developing the 'Spridget'

It seems that BMC began to look ahead to the next-generation Sprite at quite an early stage in the Frog-eye's career. Although in those days market research in the modern sense was a virtually unknown science, there is no doubt that both BMC and the Healeys took note of those – few – criticisms that had been levelled against the original Sprite, and prepared to improve the car in those areas where weaknesses had been perceived.

For instance, it was evident that the car's looks did not please all contemporary observers. The one-piece front-end and bonnet was heavy to lift, prone to shimmying which made a mockery of headlamp adjustment, and rendered access to the battery unduly difficult. But the biggest shortcoming of the Sprite was the lack of external access to the luggage area. Also, while the performance of the Frog-eye was deemed to be adequate, there was plenty of scope for improvement.

It looked as if the next Sprite was going to need re-designed front and rear ends. This meant that the body structure would become more complicated, and in turn this would inevitably increase the weight. So, to retain or improve the performance of the car, a more powerful engine was required.

Isn't it amazing what a simple face-lift can do? Despite the complicated procedure of designing the new front and rear ends separately, the Sprite Mark II of 1961 still looks all of one piece, but so very different to the Frog-eye.

No doubt it is still a good-looking little car, with a fortuitous, and probably intended, family resemblance to the soon-to-come new MGB.

NEW DESIGNS

The first task was to design a new front-end. The Healeys were asked to undertake this, and stylists Les Ireland and Doug Thorpe worked in close liaison with Donald and Geoffrey Healey. The headlamps were moved from their nacelles into the normal position in the front wings. The wings were now fixed, with a separate bonnet panel between them. The radiator grille was widened and became more rectangular in shape. At one stage, it was thought that the radiator grille might have horizontal, wavy-line bars, similar to those found on the big six-cylinder Austin-Healey (and most Austin saloon cars), but in the end the choice fell on a simple and rather neat egg-box grille which became a unique recognition point of the new Sprite. The new style front-end was mated up to an unchanged Frog-eye rear-end before being photographed for posterity.

At the same time, Syd Enever, the chief engineer of MG at Abingdon, had been asked to look into redesigning the Sprite rear-end. Oddly enough, the BMC managers had told the Healeys not to discuss the project with Enever, although he at least had been officially informed that a new front-end design was being developed at Warwick! Enever

---

Sydney Enever (born 1906) and John Thornley OBE (born 1909)
These two very different men have jointly become synonymous with MG, making an immense contribution to the company's prestige in the post-war period. They came from widely different backgrounds.

Syd Enever was a local Oxford lad who joined Morris Garages straight from school in 1921, moving to Abingdon with the young MG Car Company in 1929. John Thornley came from London, had gone to university and had joined a firm of accountants. As the owner of an M-type Midget, he was a founder member of the MG Car Club, and managed to persuade Cecil Kimber to give him a job in the service department in 1931.

Thornley became service manager in 1933, and Enever rose to become head of the experimental department. Thornley served with distinction in the army, while Enever stayed at Abingdon, helping MG's contribution to the war effort. In 1952, Thornley became MG's general manager, and two years later, Enever was appointed chief engineer and designer, when the MG drawing office was formally re-established for the first time since 1936.

Enever was responsible for the design of the new MGA which was introduced in 1955. Thornley was responsible for making more and more of them. Thornley also became a director of the parent company BMC in 1956, and was always ready to defend the interests of his beloved MG company in the highest offices of the corporation.

They were given a fresh challenge when Austin-Healey production was moved from Longbridge to Abingdon in 1957. Syd Enever became involved in the Sprite project from the early days, and contributed significantly to the development of the Sprite Mark II/Midget Mark I, at the same time master-minding the MGB project. Both Thornley and Enever remained at their posts throughout the BMC period, which saw Abingdon's production quadruple from 10,000 to 40,000 cars per year, and which saw MG and Austin-Healey become best-sellers in the US market.

Neither man was happy with the outlook for the future after the Leyland merger. Thornley had been going through a period of ill-health and decided to retire at the age of sixty, leaving the company in July 1969. Enever stayed on until he was sixty-five, retiring in May 1971 with fifty years of service to his credit.

John Thornley has continued to take an active interest in MG affairs in the years since, particularly as president of the MG Car Club. He has moved from Abingdon to Somerset, and still drives his MGB GT with the registration mark MG 1. Sydney Enever has not enjoyed the best of health, and lives quietly with his family at Oxford. It would be difficult to find two motor industry personalities more deserving of the universal respect that is given to Syd Enever and John Thornley, 'Mr MG' *and* 'Mr MG'.

The Sprite Mark II paired off with its big brother, the Austin-Healey 3000 Mark II.

felt, quite reasonably, that it would make more sense if he and Geoffrey Healey did get together to discuss what they were both doing, so they arranged an almost clandestine meeting in the neutral territory of the Morris Bodies Branch factory at Coventry.

There was no difficulty at all in establishing common ground, and from then on the joint design progressed rapidly and well. For Enever to be able to cut a boot-lid aperture in the rear-end of the Sprite, it was necessary to stiffen what remained of rear-end sheet metal. The rear wings were given additional internal bracing behind the rear wheelarches; the wheelarches were lowered and squared up, with deeper and stronger panels above the wheelarches; and a bracing panel was introduced to separate the boot from the passenger compartment. Apart from cutting in the boot-lid, the tonneau panel behind the seats was cut back for easy access to the additional luggage area there.

The simple, standard Lucas rear lights were replaced by vertical clusters, styled to follow the lines of the car, with overtones of the then fashionable Farina tailfins seen on so many other BMC cars. The new Sprite, such as it emerged during 1959–1960, bore a clear family resemblance to the major project which was engaging Syd Enever's attention

The new rear wings with their modest fins and vertical lights were very much a part of the BMC family look at the time, inspired by the Italian designer Pinin Farina . . .

. . . but it is evident that the 'new look' was restricted to the front and rear ends, with the centre section of the car being almost unchanged from the Frog-eye.

What all the fuss was about: the external boot lid. The bumpers and the overriders were still theoretically an option on the Sprite (but standard on the MG Midget). They were, however, fitted to most cars.

at the time: the new MGB, which would be launched in 1962.

PRODUCTION REALITIES

Once the styling modifications had been approved, it became the responsibility of the MG people, together with the Pressed Steel Company's body plant at Swindon to get the car into production. The tooling cost for the modifications to front- and rear-ends was considerable and was claimed to exceed the total cost of tooling-up for the Frog-eye in

The egg-crate chrome grille was the distinguishing mark of the Sprite, with the Midget having a vertical bar radiator grille. The owner of this car obviously belongs to all the right clubs!

*This US publicity photo shows the two important new features of the Sprite
Mark II: the new bonnet, and the opening boot-lid.*

1958. (This is obviously why they did not want to change it ever again!)

In fairness, the new front- and rear-ends were much more complex than they had been before. The floor, scuttle section and doors were left unchanged. The weight penalty resulting from the modified body was around 60lb (27kg). To cope with this the engine, which remained at 948cc for the time being, was mildly tuned. With flat-top instead of concave pistons, the compression ratio was increased from 8.3 to 9:1 (although the lower compression remained available to special order, being in demand in markets where high-octane petrol was not readily available).

There was a new camshaft with altered valve timing, giving a longer inlet valve opening time, and HS2 1¼in carburettors replaced the original 1⅛in carburettors (type H1). The diameter of the inlet valves was increased. The result was a modest but worthwhile gain in power, from 43bhp (net) at 5,000rpm to 46.5bhp (net) at 5,500rpm.

Torque was almost the same, 53lb ft rather than 52lb ft, but was developed at 3,000rpm rather than 3,300rpm. The flatter torque curve permitted the adoption of higher indirect gear ratios in what became known as the close-ratio gearbox, although top gear and final drive ratios remained the same.

Speedwell conversions had been very popular on the Frog-eye. This is what they proposed to do to the Mark II. Now you know why Speedwell-converted Mark II Sprites were not popular . . .

In fact, the new gear ratios were exactly those which had been found in the close-ratio box which had been optional on the Frog-eye.

Apart from the body and engine, there were very few modifications to the Sprite Mark II. One important change was that seat-belt mounting points were now built into the structure; they appeared on most BMC cars during 1961. The old-fashioned push-pull type switches on the facia were changed to BMC's latest type toggle switches, with the light switch now separated from the ignition lock, and the high beam warning light was built into the speedometer. Sealed-beam headlamps, already found on North American export Frog-eyes, were fitted also on the home market cars. There were larger, rectangular combined side lamps and front indicators with part-white, part-amber lenses, while the new rear lamp clusters had amber lenses for the indicators, and built-in reflectors.

THE MG MIDGET IS REBORN

While the new Sprite was being developed, BMC took the decision that they would

With the coming of the Mark II, the Austin-Healey Sprite badge grew wings . . .

. . . while the Sprite name-plate on the boot-lid lost its arrow.

launch an MG version of the new model as well. In that way, they would revive the famous name of MG Midget – not used on an MG model since 1954. Historically, the small, affordable sports car had been almost

exclusively MG territory. Yet the last under-1 litre model (the PB) had been discontinued in 1936, and subsequent Midgets had grown progressively in size and price, until the 1½-litre MGA of 1955 had finally appeared as a

The pierced wheels tell us that this car is one of the original 1961–1962 Mark II models with a 948cc engine; the 1,098cc car introduced in 1962 had plain wheels.

Under the new bonnet, the engine and engine bay were very similar to the Frog-eye, but a new type of air filter is an immediate recognition point.

The new bonnet on the 1961 Sprite was perhaps a little flimsy and does tend to sag a bit when it is supported on its prop.

logical progression from the last of the old-school Midgets, the TF model. Now, MG were preparing to launch an even bigger sports car, the 1.8-litre MGB, which would leave plenty of room for a smaller, cheaper model in the range.

Then, there was the question of satisfying the dealer network. The Austin and Nuffield dealer networks were as yet still largely unintegrated, and although there were exceptions, it was still unusual to find an Austin-Healey and an MG on the same show-room floor. Inevitably, MG dealers who thought it was part of their birthright to sell

Still hidden behind the heater box, the battery is marginally easier to get at than on a Frog-eye.

sports cars, had looked askance at the Sprite being exclusive to their Austin-selling rivals! In Britain and in most European markets, BMC dealer networks only began to be rationalized and integrated from 1968 onwards (an effect of the BMC-Leyland merger of that year). Only in the USA and Canada were Austin-Healeys and MGs sold through the same outlets as early as 1961.

Finally, it must be admitted that as far as the general public was concerned, MG was synonymous with sports cars, and despite the commercial and sporting successes notched up by the Austin-Healey marque since its inception in 1953, Austin-Healeys had not quite managed to capture the same degree of affection as their older rivals. By introducing an MG version of the Sprite, BMC would keep the MG enthusiasts as well as the MG dealers very happy.

It was only the Healey family who had reason to be disgruntled about this piece of badge-engineering. They would not get a royalty on the MG Midget as it did not use the Healey name, although they had been instrumental in developing the original concept for the car. It was acknowledged at the time that the Midget would undoubtedly take sales away from the Sprite, but BMC hoped that the two cars together would show an overall improvement of the production and sales figures.

Problems in the USA

In fact, something had to be done to boost the sales of BMC's sports car range. The Frog-eye Sprite had its best year in 1959 when more than 21,500 cars had been manufactured. Unfortunately, from 1959 to 1961 the US market for import cars, especially sports cars, had almost totally collapsed. This was due to the appearance of the US domestic makers' compact cars, and to a period of recession starting in the summer of 1960.

In 1959, total British car exports to the USA had topped 200,000. In 1960, the figure was little more than 130,000, and in 1961, it crumbled to 30,000. BMC were reliant on North American sales for their sports car production, and they were particularly hard hit, with Standard-Triumph being another victim of these circumstances.

In the autumn and winter of 1960 and 1961, the sports car factories at Abingdon (Austin-Healey and MG) and Canley (Triumph) were largely idle. Both manufacturers were developing new products – the Sprite/Midget, the MGB and the Austin-Healey 3000 Convertible, matched by Triumph with the TR4 and the Spitfire – and from 1962 onwards, thanks to more favourable conditions in the American market, British car exports began to pick up again.

It would have been helpful to the British motor industry if the government had shown some understanding of the problems, and although hire purchase restrictions were eased at the beginning of 1961, in the summer of that year the rate of Purchase Tax on new cars was increased from 50 to 55 per cent. As a result, the British motor industry had an extremely bad year in 1961, with production falling sharply from 1.35 million to just over 1 million. In the circumstances, it was creditable that production of the new Sprite and Midget models, which began only in March 1961, had reached a total of 17,720 cars by the end of the year.

INTRODUCTION OF THE SPRITE AND MIDGET

The normal procedure, when giving birth to twins, is that they arrive almost simultaneously. In 1959, BMC had launched the Austin and Morris Minis on the same day. Perhaps in deference to the strong loyalties for the two individual marques in question, or perhaps because BMC were being coy about badge-engineering sports cars, the debut of the Sprite Mark II and of the MG Midget were kept separate.

Return of the MG Midget: the original 1961 948cc-engined Midget, the first under-1,000cc MG for twenty-five years.

The Sprite was introduced at the beginning of June 1961, the Midget followed four weeks later. At least, it gave the company two opportunities for press coverage! While none of the contemporary press reports tried to disguise the fact that the MG Midget was basically an Austin-Healey Sprite, the motoring writers of the day were still prepared to accept the new MG on the basis of its own merits, aided undoubtedly by the impeccable MG heritage.

There was actually a total of three versions of the new car. There were two models of the Austin-Healey Sprite:

1. A standard version selling at £641.9.2 including Tax.
2. A de-luxe model selling at £655.12.6 including Tax.

The MG Midget, with a few differences and slightly better equipment, sold for £669.15.10, Tax paid. (The basic prices were £452, £462 and £472 respectively).

The facia of the 1961 Midget was identical to the Sprite, except for the MG badge and the white steering-wheel.

Twins, or Triplets?

The standard model of the Sprite was and is a rarity. It was sold only in tiny numbers, and mainly in the home market – most export cars were equipped with some or all of the deluxe items which included a rev counter, a windscreen washer, front and rear bumpers with overriders, and an adjustable passenger seat. The standard Sprite had simple vertical bumperettes at the back.

The MG Midget could be distinguished from the Sprites by its vertical-bar radiator grille, with an MG badge prominently mounted on the centre rib (the Sprite Mark II had a new, winged badge on the bonnet). The MG also had bright trim strips to the centre of the bonnet and to the sides of the car. Midget seats were of a fancier design than Sprite seats, with additional contrast colour piping, while the floor coverings were of better quality with a contrast colour 'fleck' effect. Both cars still had rubber mats to the front compartment, but featured carpets to the shelf and wheelarches behind the seats.

The Midget driver had a white steering-wheel as opposed to a black one in the Sprite, and the instruments were different, with

*The contrast-colour seat piping was typical of the Spridgets for many years,
but the flecked carpet and rubber mats only lasted for little more than one year.*

all-black dials and better calibrations on the Midget. There was a padded roll over the Midget dashboard, lacking on the Sprite, but on the other hand, a Sprite passenger had a grab handle which was absent in the Midget! Instead, the passenger could look at an MG badge with stylized wings.

Otherwise, the cars were virtually identical but were offered in different ranges of colour schemes and, although it seems totally illogical, the optional extra hard-tops were of different designs! The Sprite hard-top was similar to the Frog-eye hard-top, while the

Midget hard-top was a new design with a flatter roof and an inset rear window.

The new models were given an excellent reception by press and public alike, at home as well as in the important export markets. The Sprite Mark II was seen as a worthwhile progression from the original model – its improved looks and greatly enhanced amenity with the new bonnet and boot-lid were particularly appreciated. Most of the additional weight of the Mark II had gone over the rear wheels, but handling was found to be little different. Although the suspension felt

Extras Available for Sprite Mark II and MG Midget, 1961

- Heater and demister (or separate fresh-air unit)
- Radio (manual tuning)
- Tonneau cover, with rail and storage bag
- Cigar lighter
- Wing mirror
- Ace Mercury wheel discs
- Glassfibre hard-top
- Whitewall tyres
- Heavy-duty Dunlop Fort tyres
- Luggage rack (and wing mirror)
- Rear compartment cushion
- Locking petrol cap
- Laminated windscreen
- Twin horns
- Low compression (8.3:1) engine

The hard-tops were of different designs for the two models. An alternative hard-top, with rear quarterlights and a banana-shape rear window, was offered by Donald Healey Motors of Warwick. The rear compartment cushion was a joke, as there was no leg-room whatsoever for anyone sitting on it, nor any head-room if the hood or a hard-top was in use. Wire wheels were not offered by the factory for these models. BMC-approved seat-belts were available for fitting by dealers, together with other accessories, including some very exotic seat covers.

a little softer than on the Sprite Mark I, the ride could be bouncy, but passenger comfort was found to be adequate. The steering was much praised, although the press was now beginning to become slightly critical of BMC's gearboxes with their barely adequate synchromesh which did not extend to first gear. The cockpit was memorably described as 'surprisingly roomy', and there was 'plenty of space' in the boot.

There was very little change in the performance. A typical 0–60mph (0–100kph) time was 20 seconds, top speed was 85mph (140kph), and overall fuel consumption 33mpg (1,200km/100l). The close-ratio gearbox and the better torque characteristics gave a very marginal improvement to acceleration – so slight as to be undetectable in everyday driving. The performance of the two models was found to be identical, as could be expected.

The early road test cars submitted to the press were fitted with most of the extras and accessories offered by BMC, and it may be noted that when *The Motor* tested a more basic Midget in March 1962 they coaxed a best one-way top speed of 90mph (145kph) out of the car, together with an improved 0–60mph (0–100kph) time of 18.3 seconds. The original light-coloured Midget steering-wheel had offended *The Autocar*'s testers in August 1961, and it is amusing to note that the car tested by *The Motor* seven months later had a black steering-wheel!

THE SPRIDGET GROWS UP

There was a lot of exciting news from BMC in 1962. Most important was the launch of the Morris 1100, the Issigonis-designed family saloon with Pininfarina styling. This was destined to become Britain's best-selling car, and it took the Mini concept of transverse engine and front-wheel drive into the family car class for the first time. Then, there was the MG 1100, a badge-engineered and tuned version of the basic Morris, sharing the virtues (and failings!) of the sister car. BMC tried to rejuvenate falling saloon car sales in the USA with this MG, selling a two-door version as the MG 'Sport Sedan'.

On the sports-car side proper, there was first and foremost the new MGB, the unitary-construction 1.8-litre replacement for MGA, while the Austin-Healey 3000 went into convertible form with wind-up windows and a much improved hood.

Amongst this plethora of new models, it was almost overlooked that there were new versions of the Austin-Healey Sprite and the MG Midget. The new cars were launched on the eve of the London Motor Show and at first

Austin-Healey Sprite Mark II and MG Midget Mark I Technical Data
Engine type   BMC A-series, four cylinders in-line
Bore and stroke   62.9 × 76.2mm
Capacity   948cc
Compression ratio   9:1 (optional low compression 8.3:1)
Valves   In-line overhead valves operated by pushrods
Carburation   Two SU HS2 – 1¼in (32mm)
Maximum power   46.5 (net) at 5,500rpm
Maximum torque   53lb ft at 3,000rpm
Clutch   Single dry plate, 6¼in (16cm), hydraulically operated
Gearbox   Four-speed manual, synchromesh on 2nd, 3rd and top
Gear ratios   1st 3.2:1, 2nd 1.916:1, 3rd 1.357:1, top 1.00:1, Reverse 4.114:1
Final drive ratio   4.22:1
Front suspension:
   Front: Independent with wishbones and coil springs, lever arm shock absorbers
   Rear: Live axle with quarter-elliptic springs and radius arms, lever arm shock absorbers
Brakes   Drum brakes front and rear, 7in (18cm) drums
Steering   Rack-and-pinion
Wheels   3.5 × 13 ventilated steel disc
Tyres   5.20-13 cross-ply
Wheelbase   80in (2.03m)
Track:
   Front: 45¾in (1.16m)
   Rear: 44¾in (1.14m)
Overall length:
   Sprite with overriders: 136in (3.45m)
   Midget with overriders: 137⅝in (3.50m)
Overall width   53in (1.35m)
Overall height (hood up)   49¾in (1.26m)
Ground clearance   5in (127mm)
Fuel tank capacity   6 Imperial gallons (27 litres)
Weights:
   Kerbside weight: 1,566lb (710kg)
   Gross vehicle weight: 1,966lb (892kg)

PERFORMANCE:
Top speed   85mph (140kph)
0–60mph (0–100kph)   19 seconds
Standing ¼-mile   22 seconds
Fuel consumption   33-38mpg (1,200–1,400km/100l)

glance, were indistinguishable from their predecessors. The only external difference was that the pierced disc wheels had been replaced by plain wheels – apart from the first few of the new cars which still had the original type Sprite wheels with ventilation holes.

Further Developments

The important improvements were under the skin. The BMC A-series engine of 948cc was being phased out, and was gradually being replaced by the new 1,098cc version, with bore and stroke increased from 62.9 × 76.2mm to 64.6 × 83.7mm. This engine had made its debut in the Morris 1100 in August 1962, and was soon installed also in the Morris Minor 1000, the Austin A40 Farina, and the Austin A35 van, apart from in the Spridgets.

In the small sports cars, still featuring two SU HS2 carburettors, the new engine had a

On their Motor Show stand in 1962, Donald Healey showed this Mark II
Sprite with their own hard-top and wire-wheel conversion.

compression ratio of 8.9:1, and developed a healthy 56bhp at 5,750rpm. The maximum torque figure was 62lb ft at 3,250rpm. Translated into road performance, it meant that the Spridget now had a genuine 88mph (140kph) top speed, with over 90mph (145kph) being possible in favourable circumstances, with 0–60mph (0–100kph) being accomplished in less than 17 seconds. Fuel consumption was slightly adversely effected, at around 30mpg (1,100km/100l) overall.

Together with the new engine came an extensively revised gearbox, with a new stronger casing and, most importantly, much more effective baulk-ring synchromesh in place of the original cone-type synchromesh – although BMC still refused to provide synchromesh on first gear. The ratios were unchanged from the previous model. The third

major improvement was the fitting of disc brakes on the front wheels, supplied by Lockheed, and of 8¼in (209mm) in diameter. These greatly improved the stopping power of the car, especially as the fading tendencies to which the drum-braked models had been prone had now been largely eliminated.

The interior trim was greatly improved, with better-upholstered seats now of a design common to both Sprite and Midget. There were better quality door casings, and carpet to both front and rear compartment, again found on both models and in plain colours without the 'fleck' effect. The dashboard was given padded rolls to top and bottom edges on both cars, and the same type of Smiths instruments was also found on both models. The rev counter was now of the electronic type, which avoided the troublesome mechanical drive from the rear of the dynamo found

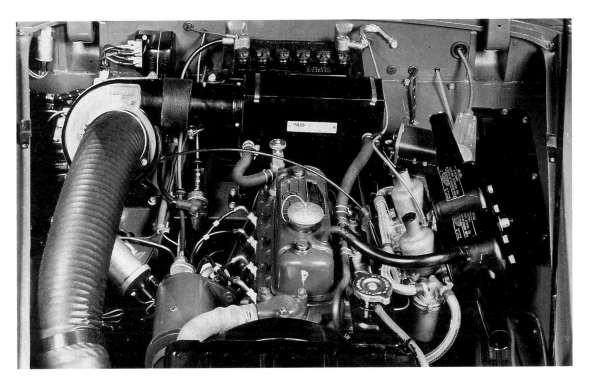

Under the bonnet of the MG Midget Mark I.

on previous models. There were revisions to the range of colour schemes (still slightly different on the two models), and in addition to the well-established trim colours of red, black and blue, a brown trim colour called 'Hazelnut' appeared.

The standard Sprite model was discontinued, so from now on all Sprites came complete with rev counter, windscreen washer, front and rear bumpers, and both seats adjustable. Basic prices were increased by £23 for both models, keeping the slight price differential between Sprite and Midget. Total prices (tax paid) on introduction were £668 for the Sprite and £682 for the Midget.

Within a month of the launch, Purchase Tax was slashed to 25 per cent, which brought Spridget prices down to their lowest ever figures: £587 for the Sprite, and £599 for the Midget. The list of extras offered for the revised cars was virtually the same but, for the first time, wire wheels became available

as an option, and the Midget type hard-top was now standardized on both models.

Although the 1,098cc-engined cars were given new chassis prefixes (*see* Appendix 1), their designations were not officially changed but they were sometimes referred to as the Sprite 1100 and Midget 1100 models. They are now sometimes known as the Sprite Mark II½ and Midget Mark I½! There would, in due course, be Sprite Mark III and Midget Mark II models . . .

THE RIVAL

The outlook for the two new models was good, but would have been better still had it not been for the fact that in that same Motor Show of October 1962, BMC's great rival for the sports car market, Standard-Triumph, introduced the first Triumph Spitfire – always the main, and for a long time the only

Will it all fit in? The young lady looks a little worried that it might not. You really need soft luggage to use the Spridget boot to the full.

rival to the Spridget. Based on the Triumph Herald chassis with its swing-axle type rear suspension, the original Spitfire 4 had a 1,147cc engine developing 63bhp.

The new Triumph had a top speed of 92–93mph (148–150kph) and better acceleration than the Spridget. It had a roomier and more comfortable cockpit, and boasted wind-up windows rather than the loose sidescreens of the BMC car. Compared to the Spridget, its main failings were the dubious handling induced by its swing-axle suspension, and a dashboard with centrally-mounted instru-

ments. It was also more expensive, at £641 after the reduction in Purchase Tax. Comparable prices in the USA in 1963 were: Sprite $1,875; Midget $1,945; and Spitfire $2,199.

The Spitfire made an immediate impression in the marketplace, and in its first full year of production comfortably outsold the Sprite and Midget together. Indeed it continued to do so in most years between 1963 and 1979. The great rivalry was on, and no doubt the Spitfire spurred BMC on to make even further improvements to the Sprite and Midget models.

Austin-Healey Sprite Mark II and MG Midget Mark I, 1,098cc Technical Data

Engine type   BMC A-series, four cylinders in-line
Bore and stroke   64.6 × 83.7mm
Capacity   1,098cc
Compression ratio   8.9:1 (optional low compression 8:1)
Valves   In-line overhead valves operated by pushrods
Carburation   Two SU HS2 – 1¼in (32mm)
Maximum power   56bhp (net) at 5,750rpm
Maximum torque   62lb ft at 3,250rpm
Clutch   Single dry plate, 7¼in (18cm), hydraulically operated
Gearbox   Four-speed manual, synchromesh on 2nd, 3rd and top
Gear ratios   1st 3.2:1, 2nd 1.916:1, 3rd 1.357:1, top 1.00:1, reverse 4.120:1
Final drive ratio   4.22:1
Suspension:
    Front: Independent with wishbones and coil springs, lever arm shock absorbers
    Rear: Live axle with quarter-elliptic springs and radius arms, lever arm shock absorbers
Brakes:
    Front: 8¼in (21cm) discs
    Rear: 7in (18cm) drums
Steering   Rack-and-pinion
Wheels   3.5 × 13 disc wheels (optional: 4J × 13 60-spoke wire wheels)
Tyres   5.20-13 cross-ply
Wheelbase   80in (2.03m)
Track:
    Front: 46⁷⁄₁₆in (1.18m)
    Rear: 44¾in (1.14m) – disc wheels; 45¼in (1.15m) – wire wheels
Overall length:
    Sprite: 136in (3.45m)
    Midget: 137⅝in (3.50m)
Overall width   53in (1.35m)
Overall height (hood up)   49¾in (1.26m)
Ground clearance   5in (127mm)
Fuel tank capacity   6 Imperial gallons (27 litres)
Weights:
    Kerbside weight: 1,566lb (710kg)
    Gross vehicle weight: 2,090lb (948kg)

PERFORMANCE:
Top speed   88mph (141.5kph)
0–60mph (0–100kph)   17 seconds
Standing ¼-mile   21 seconds
Fuel consumption   31–37mpg (1,100–1,300km/100l)

5 Better, and Bigger...

The years 1963–1969 saw almost continuous, worthwhile development of the Spridget cars. Thereafter, the design seemed to stagnate, and such modifications as were made during the 1970s seemed to be either irrelevant or retrograde. By the end of the 1960s, to put it bluntly, the Spridget had come to the end of its useful design life. The Midget did continue in production for another ten years (the Sprite being discontinued in 1971), and carried on performing respectably in terms of sales. Yet, by the standards of the 1970s, it was an anachronism, and not one that most contemporary observers could begin to feel nostalgic about.

Although there was no shortage of ideas for Spridget replacements, BMC never did manage to get a rejuvenated small sports car into production before 1968, and after the merger of Leyland and BMC in that year, the chance of seeing a Spridget replacement in production became remote.

The 1963 models had benefited from the introduction of the 1,098cc engine, the improved gearbox and the disc front brakes. The next steps in the evolution of the Spridget tackled those areas where the car was most deficient compared to the rival newcomer, the Triumph Spitfire.

MORE COMFORT...

First came the introduction in March 1964 of the Sprite Mark III and Midget Mark II models. Most of the improvements on these cars centred on the aspects of comfort and convenience, but the engines were also modified to give that little bit of extra power which would keep the performance on par with the Spitfire. As yet, however, the engine capacity remained the same at 1,098cc.

The biggest single modification on the Sprite Mark III and its MG sibling was a new rear suspension. The old quarter-elliptic springs with radius arms for locating the rear axle were replaced by conventional semi-elliptic springs. Among the advantages of the new suspension were cited better axle location and reduced unsprung weight. Strangely enough, these had been the precise reasons for using the quarter-elliptic springs in the first place (*see* Chapter 2)!

The truth of it was that since the rear-end of the body structure had been stiffened up to accept the opening boot-lid in 1961, it had no longer been necessary to feed rear-suspension stresses directly into the main floor pan. The new rear suspension also permitted greater axle travel so it became possible to use softer springs which made the Spridget's ride much smoother. The new rear suspension also gave a better axle location and so improved the handling as well as the comfort of the car.

...MORE CONVENIENCE...

While the new rear suspension looked after comfort, convenience was greatly improved by the new wind-up windows, replacing the detachable sidescreens. A little bit of fiddling

(Right)   The Midget Mark II and Sprite Mark III were introduced in 1964. They can be easily identified by their combination of the old-type pack-away hood with the wind-down windows, quarter lights and new windscreen.

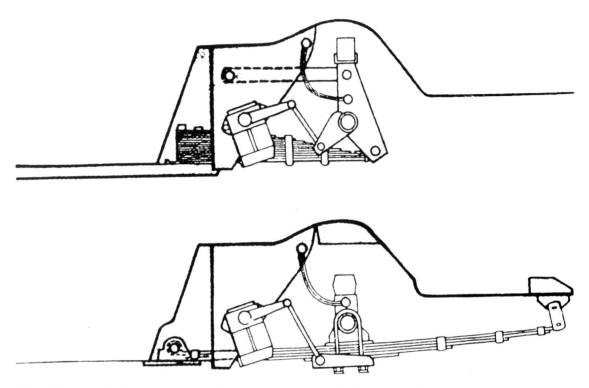

The differences in the rear suspension between the quarter-elliptic springs of the original Spridgets (above) and the semi-elliptic springs introduced in 1964 (below).

was necessary to install the window-winding gear in the thin doors without losing too much precious elbow room. With the aid of curved glass for the side windows, however, this was largely accomplished, the only detrimental effect being the loss of the door pockets.

In addition to the drop glasses, there were small swivelling quarter lights at the front. The main reason for adopting these was that the drop windows needed a channel to run in, there being no other window frames. The windscreen frame was improved and the rear-view mirror was moved from the top of the scuttle to a tie-rod between the upper and lower windscreen frame, so the position of the mirror could be adjusted to suit driver preference.

The doors were fitted with exterior handles for the first time, of the push-button type, and with key-operated locks to both doors. The original interior string-pull releases for the door locks were replaced by handles with a separate locking catch. They were recessed at the rear of the doors, making them slightly awkward to reach. The seats were very similar to the superseded models, but the door casings were obviously all new, while there was a completely new facia, as well as a new steering-wheel.

Instead of being covered in Vynide, the facia was finished in black crackle-finish paint, similar to that of the MGB. The instrument panel had the two main dials either side of the steering-column, slightly angled towards each other, while the two smaller gauges were now in the centre of the facia together with the switch gear. The facia panel was recessed in front of the passenger, and there was a small parcel shelf under this

The accessory manufacturers were still busy. Cobramold Limited at Stanstead airfield in Essex offered this Spridget hard-top in 1963.

In 1964, the Sprite Mark III (and Midget Mark II) were given wind-down windows, a new facia, and wire wheels became optional.

Apart from the distinctive MG style radiator grille, the 1960s Midgets were distinguished from contemporary Sprites by their chrome trim strips, down the sides of the car as well as on the bonnet. The external door handles were another improvement introduced in 1964.

Austin-Healey Sprite Mark III and MG Midget Mark II Technical Data

Engine type   BMC A-series, four cylinders in-line
Bore and stroke   64.6 × 83.7mm
Capacity   1,098cc
Compression ratio   8.9:1 (optional low compression 8.1:1)
Valves   In-line overhead valves operated by pushrods
Carburation   Two SU HS2 – 1¼in (32mm)
Maximum power   59bhp (net) at 5,750rpm
Maximum torque   65lb ft at 3,500rpm
Clutch   Single dry plate, 7¼in (18cm), hydraulically operated
Gearbox   Four-speed manual, synchromesh on 2nd, 3rd and top
Gear ratios   1st 3.2:1, 2nd 1.916:1, 3rd 1.357:1, top 1.00:1, reverse 4.120:1
Final drive ratio   4.22:1
Suspension:
  Front: Independent with wishbones and coil springs, lever arm shock absorbers
  Rear: Live axle with semi-elliptic springs, lever arm shock absorbers
Brakes:
  Front: 8¼in (21cm) discs
  Rear: 7in (18cm) drums
Steering   Rack-and-pinion
Wheels   3.5 × 13 disc wheels (optional: 4J × 13 60-spoke wire wheels)
Tyres   5.20-13 cross-ply
Wheelbase   80in (2.03m)
Track:
  Front: 46⁵⁄₁₆in (1.18m)
  Rear: 44¾in (1.14m) – disc wheels; 45¼in (1.15m) – wire wheels
Overall length   137⅜in (3.49m)
Overall width   54⅞in (1.39m) – disc wheels; 56½in (1.43m) – wire wheels
Overall height (hood up)   48½in (1.23m)
Ground clearance   5in (127mm)
Fuel tank capacity   6 Imperial gallons (27 litres)
Weights:
  Kerbside weight: 1,530lb (694kg)
  Gross vehicle weight: 1,946lb (883kg)

PERFORMANCE:
Top speed   92mph (148kph)
0–60mph (0–100kph)   14 seconds
Standing ¼-mile   20 seconds
Fuel consumption   29–36mpg (1,000–1,300km/100l)

The Midget Mark II interior, showing the new facia and steering-wheel.

side of the dashboard, to compensate for the lost door pockets. The steering-wheel was also inspired by the MGB: a handsome affair with three paired wire spokes. Smaller changes to the control layout involved the previously separate starter pull giving way to a key-operated starter, while the indicators were operated by a stalk on the steering-column rather than a switch on the panel.

...AND MORE POWER

The engine was somewhat modified in the new models. The crankshaft was stiffer, with the main bearing journals increased in size to 2in. The inlet valves were increased in size, and the porting improved, while a

new four-branch exhaust manifold also contributed to greater engine efficiency. An SU electric fuel pump replaced the mechanical type found on earlier models. The compression ratio was unchanged at 8.9:1. The maximum power output was now 59bhp at 5,750rpm, while the maximum torque was improved to 65lb ft at 3,500rpm.

With a top speed of 93mph (148kph) and a 0–60mph (0–100kph) time just below 15 seconds, the Sprite Mark III or Midget Mark II would just keep a Triumph Spitfire at bay. On the other hand, the Spridget's overall fuel consumption at 29mpg (1,000km/100l) was slightly greater than the Spitfire's, and the small 6-gallon (27-litre) tank was attracting adverse comments. It was a sign of the times that the new Spridget was slightly slower

Externally there was no difference between the 948cc and the 1,098cc Midget Mark I. This is the 1,098cc version, fitted with the Ace wheel discs which were optional on the early Midgets.

than the four-seater (but admittedly more expensive) Mini-Cooper 'S' with its 1,071cc engine. The prices for the latest Spridgets on introduction in 1964 were £611 for the Sprite, £623 for the Midget, while the Spitfire was still offered at £641, and the Mini-Cooper 'S' cost £695 (all prices including Purchase Tax).

TRIUMPH'S RESPONSE

Meanwhile, the appeal of the Triumph Spitfire was enhanced as Triumph offered wire wheels, a hard-top and an overdrive as options. This last feature was very much one

up on the competition. While overdrive was a popular fitment on the Big Healey and the MGB, it was never available on the Spridget, allegedly because there was no room behind the gearbox, and it would have been too complicated and costly to re-design the floor-pan structure to accommodate an overdrive.

In 1965, the Spitfire went into its Mark II form with another 3bhp from the 1,147cc engine, although top speed as measured by magazine road testers stayed the same, at 92mph (148kph). The revised Spitfire also benefited from more comfortably uphol-stered seats, better interior trim and full floor carpeting. Its rear suspension, instrument

The boot-lid badges also followed standard MG practice. The three-piece octagonal badge was later replaced by a cheaper one-piece plastic badge.

introduce the 1,275cc Sprite Mark IV and Midget Mark III, and even so this was not the Cooper 'S' engine.

This made sense, in as much as the 'S' type engine was a rather specialized unit not totally suitable for mass-market production. The new Spridget engine did not, for instance, have the Nitralloy crankshaft or the extra cylinder-head studs found on the Cooper engine. In fact both block and head were fairly substantially re-designed for ease of production, and the new engine could be easily identified by the absence of tappet covers.

The Midget used the same badge as the chrome-bumper MGB, with the classic octagon set in a shield. Various colours have been used for the MG badge over the years, but silver and red are the most commonly seen these days.

panel and appearance were unchanged, but the price went up to £666 including Tax.

The rivals were well matched, and after the first sensational year of Spitfire production (1963 saw almost 21,000 Spitfires produced, against 16,500 Spridgets), the Abingdon twins were slightly narrowing the difference. (For complete comparative production figures, *see* Appendix 1, page 215). It may also be noted that production of the Midget was gradually increasing at the expense of the Sprite, 1964 being the first year when more Midgets than Sprites were made.

AND 1,275CC AT LAST...

Ever since the first Mini-Cooper (of 997cc) had been launched in 1961, comparisons had been made between this car and the Sprid-gets. When the Mini-Cooper 'S' was launched with a 1,071cc engine in 1963 and received the first 1,275cc version of the A-series engine in 1964, many commentators became rather impatient with BMC for not fitting the Mini-Cooper 'S' type engine in the Spridget as well. But not before October 1966 did BMC

Normally the wire wheels would be painted silver, and it was very unusual to have them chrome-plated. The knock-on spinners were already illegal in some countries by the 1960s, and would eventually disappear altogether for safety reasons, being replaced by octagonal wheel nuts.

Bore and stroke of the 1,275cc engine were 70.6 × 81.3mm, and with a compression ratio of 8.8:1 (lower than the Cooper 'S') output was 64bhp at 5,800rpm, 11bhp less than the Cooper. The maximum torque was improved to 72lb ft at 3,000rpm. Although the more powerful engine could have pulled a higher final drive, the 4.22 ratio was retained, and gearbox ratios were also unchanged. The top speed of the 1,275cc Spridgets was a genuine 95mph (155kph), and the 0–60mph (0–100kph) acceleration time was usefully reduced, to 13 seconds. Fuel economy remained unaffected, with an overall consumption on test of around 30mpg (1,100km/100l).

The engine was not the only new thing in the Sprite Mark IV and Midget Mark III. There was a new Borg & Beck 6.5in diaphragm spring clutch, and there were separate hydraulic reservoirs for the clutch and

brakes. This simplified the situation as regards those models exported to countries such as France which required a transparent brake-fluid reservoir. It would also make it simpler to convert the cars to dual-circuit braking systems in the future.

THE CONVERTIBLE-TYPE HOOD

Another enormous improvement, making the cars much more suitable for all-weather motoring, was a new convertible-type hood. Since 1961, all Spridgets had had the infamous 'pack-away' type hood which, basically speaking, was a kit bag full of bits that needed assembly every time you wanted to put up the hood. Now, the hood and hood-frame were permanently attached in the ton-

With the Mark IV Sprite, there was a much-improved hood, and the 1,275cc engine.

neau area behind the seats, and once the hood cover had been removed, raising the hood was a simple, almost one-handed operation. Folding it was more complicated, as the hood fabric still needed to be pulled clear of the frame and furled properly so as to avoid damaging the rear window.

The new hood was only available in black, coloured hoods had disappeared for good, and all hard-tops were now also black. Similarly, although a few black and white cars were still fitted with red trim, most cars now had black trim with pale grey contrast piping on the seats, and black interiors soon became universal. The seat patterns were slightly changed.

However, there was a price to be paid for the improvements. Basic prices went up by £40, their highest increase so far, and the

new models cost £672 for the Sprite, and £684 for the Midget (including Purchase Tax). In fact, the Midget was now slightly more expensive than the Spitfire Mark II which cost £678.

THE SPITFIRE MARK III

While BMC had stolen a march on Triumph by getting the 1.3-litre version of their small sports car into production first, it did not take Triumph long to catch up. The Spitfire Mark III was launched in March 1967, with a 1,296cc engine developing 75bhp, and with a new frontal appearance resulting from the bumper being raised to meet new American bumper height requirements. The revised Spitfire sold for £717, and turned out not to be any quicker than the new Spridgets, with a top speed of just about 95mph (153kph).

It is quite entertaining to look back through the price lists of the 1960s and find that the heater was still quoted as an optional extra, and indeed would remain so until mid-1968. Other extras now available on the Spridget included an oil cooler, a headlamp flasher and a front anti-roll bar, which had all appeared in late 1964 and which were all quite useful and desirable. During 1967, the option of Road Speed tyres was quoted, but in early 1968, for the first time Dunlop SP radial tyres became available as an optional extra on the Spridget, although undoubtedly many private owners had fitted them previously.

THE AMERICAN REVOLUTION

In 1965, the young American lawyer Ralph Nader published his book, *Unsafe at Any Speed.* The book was intended as a searing indictment of the American motor industry – largely as a result of a series of 'inexplicable' accidents which had occurred involving General Motors' first compact car, the rear-engined Chevrolet Corvair of 1959. However, *Unsafe at Any Speed* ended up as a general lambasting of the disregard for safety and anti-pollution measures shown by the motor industry world-wide.

Rarely has a book had greater impact on an industry. Nader's accumulation of facts was

The Midget Mark III interior, showing the door trims adopted for cars with wind-down windows, also the neat hood cover for the convertible-type hood.

taken extremely seriously by the US authorities (particularly in California where the smog generated by car exhausts had long been an unpleasant feature of the Los Angeles basin) but also on Federal levels. In spite of protests from Detroit, the first Federal standards for automobile safety and emissions were formulated and were brought into force from 1 January 1968.

Inevitably, the new American regulations had a knock-on effect in Europe. The European manufacturers selling cars in the USA were obliged to modify their cars, or pull out of this still potentially lucrative market. Some European countries, notably Sweden, West Germany and Switzerland, also began

to formulate and enforce their own standards, although it would take another ten years before a reasonable degree of harmonization was achieved through the efforts of the much-maligned Common Market bureaucrats at Strasburg and Brussels.

Improvements

For BMC there was no question. While they decided to stop production of the ageing Austin-Healey 3000 rather than spend time and money on modifying it to meet the new standards, the American market was still tremendously important for their sports car sales. Therefore, the MGB, the new MGC,

The instruments were by now common to both Sprite and Midget. An electronic rev counter was fitted, abolishing the tiresome mechanical drive. The rear-view mirror could be adjusted up and down the central strengthening brace for the windscreen.

and the Sprite/Midget models were all suitably modified for the US market in late 1967. For the first time, the Spridget was fitted with a slightly different engine in North American export models. The actual modifications compared to the other markets were still quite modest, and performance of the North American version remained practically unimpaired. The 1968 US models of the Spridget engines still developed 62bhp, a reduction of only 2bhp compared to the standard models, and the top speed was quoted as 92mph (148kph). Worse was to come!

The other modifications undertaken to bring the Spridget into line with US regulations were all really quite sensible, and were items which have long since become standard on cars world-wide. One suspects that the only reason why BMC did not add these features to all models was to keep down the cost of the cars in the home market and non-US export markets, as long as there was no statutory requirements for extra safety features in these markets.

The 1968 models for North America were fitted with dual-circuit brakes, an energy-absorbing steering-column, and a rather clumsily designed padded dashboard which did, however, bring all instruments in front of the driver. There were two-speed wipers, now with an electric windscreen washer. There was an improved heater/demister with a more efficient high-speed blower. Flashing hazard warning lights were fitted. There was a brake-failure warning light. Padded sun visors were fitted, and other standard features included three-point seat-belts and a wing mirror on the driver's side.

Some improvements were introduced simultaneously on home market cars as well, including two reversing lights fitted as standard, a negative-earth electrical system, and safety-motivated black plastic interior door handles and window-winders. If wire wheels were specified, they now had octagonal style spinners instead of eared knock-ons – these had been required for many European export

The gearlever turret should be body colour (white on this car). Apart from a non-standard gearlever knob, this provident Midget owner has also fitted a handbrake lock. On the Midget, you got an MG badge on the dashboard; there was no Austin-Healey badge on the Sprite dashboard.

markets for ten years, and were found on most wire-wheeled cars for the USA from 1966 onwards.

Later modifications for the North American markets would be more drastic. They included ever more emasculated engines to cope with stricter emissions control regulations, and the infamous safety bumper regulations which resulted in such a major change to the appearance of the MG Midget in 1974. In 1969, there was another important change as far as marketing the Spridget in North America was concerned. With the demise of the Big Healey and the introduction of the 1300-based Austin America model, it was felt more appropriate to sell all sports cars in North America under the MG banner. At the end of the 1969 model year, the Austin-Healey Sprite was completely withdrawn from the North American markets and soon after also from other export markets. This had an immediate impact on the production figures of this model as will be clear from the detailed statistics found in Appendix 2. For the benefit of loyal enthusiasts in the home market, the Sprite continued in limited production until 1971, but from then on, the MG Midget was in sole occupancy of the roost.

FATEFUL HOUR: THE LEYLAND MERGER

After fifteen years of mixed fortunes, time ran out for the BMC combine in 1967. That year saw a dramatic decline in their home market share, and the corporation was heading for an overall loss at the end of the financial year. Harold Wilson's Labour government was becoming seriously worried about the state of the British motor industry. In January 1967, the American Chrysler Corporation extended their minority interest in the ailing Rootes Group to a complete take-over. The subsequent loss of one of the 'big five' UK producers to foreign interests did not go down well with a government which was politically committed to further the interests of the British worker.

To those in the know, it was becoming obvious that the biggest UK manufacturer, BMC, was heading for trouble. The major challenge obviously came from Ford, but during the 1960s imported cars gained an increasing share of the market, and there was a great deal of anxiety that for a number of different reasons, BMC was slipping behind European competitors such as Volkswagen, Renault and Fiat. At the same time, the go-ahead Lancashire truck manufacturer of Leyland had established itself in an enviable position. Thanks to a series of take-overs and mergers, they now held an interest in the car industry through acquisitions of Standard-Triumph in 1961, and Rover-Alvis in 1966.

THE GREAT SOLUTION

Anxious to find a solution to the problems troubling BMC, and anxious to create a united, strong British motor industry combine to repel the attrition from American or European conglomerates, the government hit upon the panacea of a merger between ailing giant BMC and thrusting, successful new-comer Leyland. They found that the Leyland management and its leading light, Donald Stokes, were receptive to the ideas. Indeed, there had already been some previous negotiations between BMC and Leyland in 1964, and again in 1966, but they had at first foundered on the question how to value the two companies' share holdings and, subsequently, on the question of personalities.

On those previous occasions, it had seemed that BMC would be the dominant partner if it came to a merger. With the BMC fortunes now sharply reversed, Leyland was favoured to make a simple take-over of British Motor Holdings, as the group had been officially known since the merger of BMC and Jaguar in 1966. Not only was Leyland now seen as the dominant partner in the eventual merger, but Stokes was favoured as chief executive in preference to the gentlemanly but

Donald Stokes (born 1914, created Lord Stokes of Leyland 1969)

It can now be rather difficult to find anyone who will admit to having ever liked Lord Stokes or who has a good word for him. Traditionally, he has been cast as the villain in the story of MG after the BMC–Leyland merger. But this is not a fair assessment and his real achievements should not be overlooked.

Born in Kent, Donald Stokes joined Leyland Motors Limited as an apprentice in 1930, and after war-time service (where he ended as a Lieutenant-Colonel) he was appointed the company's export sales manager in 1947. His first big break came when he clinched a deal to supply buses to Cuba, and from 1949 he was in charge of all Leyland sales. By 1958, he had become a director of the company.

In 1961, Leyland took over the ailing Standard-Triumph Company in Coventry. Together with Stanley Markland, Stokes moved to Coventry to sort out the mess. When Markland resigned at the end of 1963, Stokes became chairman of Standard-Triumph, as well as managing director and deputy chairman of the parent Leyland company. Stokes was the youngest and most dynamic member of the Leyland board at this time, and the remarkable turn-around in Triumph's fortunes during the 1960s must very largely be credited to his leadership. In 1965, Stokes was knighted, and in 1967 he succeeded Lord Black as chairman of Leyland.

Talks between Leyland and BMC had been going on and off since 1964, but it was only when the Wilson government took an interest in the matter in 1967 that serious negotiations began. When asked directly by the Prime Minister, both Donald Stokes and BMC's George Harriman agreed that a merger would be 'in the national interest'. The agreement that was eventually reached in January 1968 may have been in the national interest, but appeared to be rather more in Leyland's than in BMC's favour.

Stokes became chairman and managing director of the new British Leyland Motor Corporation. As it turned out, sorting out BMC was a much more complicated job than it had been at Standard-Triumph. While Stokes remained a popular figure with the government, the media and the public, he was not well liked or respected within the former BMC companies. If, indeed, he were as predisposed towards Triumph as most commentators have asserted, can one blame him for this? After all, Triumph was a success story by 1969, but BMC was a disaster area.

That British Leyland failed is no single individual's fault. The cards were stacked against the company and the final blow came with the oil crisis in 1973. British Leyland went into the red, and the government asked Lord Ryder to write his report, which resulted in the nationalization in 1975. Stokes was replaced as chairman, and after a brief period as honorary president, retired from the company to which he had given forty-five years of service.

ineffectual BMH chairman, George Harriman (who had replaced Leonard Lord in 1961). While everyone liked the idea of creating one big British motor manufacturer ('in the national interest', as it was said) Stokes had particular reason to be happy, in view of what Graham Turner in *The Leyland Papers* called 'his ambition for himself and his company'.

LEYLAND'S TRIUMPH

The merger which was finally concluded after some tense negotiations in January 1968,

was a complete victory from the Leyland point of view – inevitable in view of BMC's weak position at the time. The new company was named British Leyland Motor Corporation, or BLMC for short. The initial public reaction was largely favourable. The statistics were impressive on paper: here was a great new British company, the fifth-largest private enterprise in the country and, apart from Volkswagen, the biggest motor manufacturer outside the USA.

Before the merger could be ratified by the shareholders of the two companies, it became apparent that the state of affairs within BMC was worse than at first apparent. The outcome was that both George Harriman and his able deputy, Joe Edwards, were forced to resign, giving Donald Stokes complete control of BLMC. Because of personality clashes, and because of the very different outlook and styles of management of the two companies, the merger began to go sour from the very early days.

One of the fundamental premises of the merger was that the combined model range of BMC and Leyland should be severely rationalized. Inevitably, this would have its effects also on the new corporation's sports car programme, where the Austin-Healey/MG range would have to mesh with the Triumph range. The thought of this sent shivers down the backbone of loyal Abingdon

employees. They had no illusions about their future and were quite certain that the Leyland management was totally Triumph-orientated, and would as soon see the Austin-Healey and MG range discontinued and the Abingdon factory closed.

The worries at the time of the merger probably contributed to the worsening health of John Thornley, MG's much respected and able general manager since 1952, and an MG employee and enthusiast since 1930. His health caused him to take early retirement in 1969 (although with continued involvement in MG matters), and two years later Syd Enever also retired. Without their two guiding lights, the future of Abingdon and MG looked very bleak indeed.

6 'Leylandization'

As suggested in the previous chapter, during the 1960s BMC's development of the Spridget models had been careful and deliberate, each new modification representing an actual improvement of the car. For a little while, this policy was continued. During 1968, a number of smaller modifications was carried out. Reversing lamps were fitted as standard, and the electrical system was converted to negative earth. Interior door handles and window-winders were replaced by safety-types in black plastic. Knock-ons on wire wheels were replaced by octagonal spinners.

In mid-1968, the 1969 model year was heralded by the introduction of a modified colour range which, for the first time, meant that the Sprite and Midget were available in exactly the same colour range as the MGB Roadster. The interior trim was also modified, with a new design of door casings and a different grade vinyl upholstery for the seats. The basic seat pattern was not changed, but the piping was now in the main seat colour and no longer in contrasting light grey.

Also new for the 1969 model year were the auxiliary gauges. These were no longer rim-lit but back-lit, with new graphics and, in the case of the water thermometer read in Centigrade as opposed to Fahrenheit (Centigrade thermometers had long been available on export cars). The rear axle ratio was raised to 3.9:1. There was a new type of petrol gauge sender unit in the tank, and a new cross-flow radiator with reduced coolant capacity as part of a semi-sealed cooling system which incorporated an expansion tank. During 1968, the heater had finally become standard on home market cars.

More cars were now being fitted with an oil cooler, a front anti-roll bar, or a headlamp flasher, which had all been added to the list of options when the Sprite Mark IV/Midget Mark III had been introduced in 1966. One of the distinguishing MG Midget features had, however, been lost: the chrome trim strip to the bonnet was no longer fitted, having been discontinued in late 1968. A different type of hard-top had appeared, fitted with rear quarter lights and very similar in style to the MGB optional hard-top.

A FACE-LIFT FOR THE SPRIDGET

The Sprite and Midget remained largely unchanged for the first eighteen months after the BMC-Leyland merger. The first big post-Leyland face-lift occurred for the 1970 model year. The new cars went into production in August 1969 for a public debut just before the London Motor Show in October. While there were no changes to the Mark designations, there were new chassis number prefixes for the first time since 1966, so that the Sprite Mark IV became the H-AN10 model and the Midget Mark III became the G-AN5 model. (Sprite brochures now referred to the car as the 'Mark Four' and Midget brochures omitted the Mark number altogether.)

There was very little in the way of mechanical change and the engines, which had been introduced in their latest up-dated form in late 1967, were carried forward both on the North American Midget (engine type 12CD) and on 'rest-of-the world' Midgets and Sprites (engine type 12CE). However, during 1970 North American engines were fitted with evaporative loss control and became type 12CJ.

The major changes were external, and largely cosmetic. There was a new grille, common to both models – a matt black egg-crate, well recessed in the grille opening, with thin chrome-plated strips surrounding it, and either the MG badge or a new Austin-Healey Sprite badge in the centre. The front bumper was slimmer, and the overriders had rubber inserts. The full-width rear bumper was replaced by two quarter bumpers (also with rubber-faced overriders) and a mounting for a square rear number plate in the centre. The number-plate lamps were built into the inner ends of the quarter bumpers. The sills were painted black with a chrome trim strip, and bore prominent name plates – either Sprite or Midget – at the front end. There were corporate British Leyland badges on each front wing, in front of the doors.

Wire wheels still remained an option, but the standard steel-disc wheels with bright hub caps were replaced by the first generation of Rostyle wheels. These were pressed-steel wheels made by Rubery Owen – hence the 'Ro' in Rostyle – and their 'style' was highly debatable. Styled they certainly were, but not to everyone's taste. They were supposed to look as if they might be cast-alloy wheels and have indeed fooled some casual observers. They had eight square ventilation holes, the centre of the wheel was painted black and the rim silver, the wheel nuts were not covered by a hub cap and there was only a small bright plug-type finisher for the centre aperture.

A change which only affected the MG Midget was that this model now lost also its side chrome-trim strips. Altogether, it

The 1970 MG Midget in its 'Leyland'-type decor, complete with the original Rostyle wheels, and the short-lived unpopular matt black windscreen frame.

The 1973 model Midget featured the round rear wheelarches and the second type of Rostyle wheels.

appeared as a dead ringer for the Sprite (badges and name plates excepted). The windscreen and quarter-light frames now sported a black anodized finish. This was not a popular change, however, and after only a few months, bright finished frames were reintroduced. The rear-light clusters had new lenses which somehow looked much bigger and bulkier, and which were in fact common to the MGB model. The front side and indicator lamps were mounted slightly lower down, to compensate for the thinner bumpers.

INTERIOR CHANGES

Inside, there was plenty of change as well. Even if the Spridgets had never been avail-

New Colours

Perhaps the most obvious change of all to the 1970 model year cars was that there was an almost completely new colour range. The first Leyland colours were introduced (with code numbers prefixed BLVC for British Leyland Vehicle Colour) and within another year, the last of the old BMC colours would disappear. Probably the most garish was Bronze Yellow, a dark yellow hinting at the fashionable orange and, of course, they had to choose a Bronze Yellow Midget to illustrate the new brochure. Why was it that the 1970s BLVC colours seemed so much more contrived in their shades, and their names, than the 1960s BMC colours? Tartan Red and Mineral Blue seemed nice and straightforward and understandable, but what were we to make of Bracken, Tundra, Mirage, Aconite or Bedouin?

From the rear, the slim quarter bumpers with their rubber-faced overriders were a recognition point of the new 1970 model year cars. Supposedly used to facilitate the fitting of American license plates, they meant that it was preferable to use a square rear number plate in the home market. Note also the one-piece MG badge on the boot-lid.

able with leather upholstery, the illusion had been there, with traditional seat patterns complete with stitched channels and piping. The new Spridget seats had what was too obviously vinyl upholstery. This came with a heat-formed pattern, of which the most obvious feature was a narrow centre-band with a ladder-like pattern. On the bonus side, adjustable seat squabs were now fitted as standard, and the squabs were prepared for

As a result of the Leyland face-lift in 1969, the Midget received a new radiator grille, matt black sills, new bumpers and new seats. This car is fitted with the original type of Rostyle wheels. A white car of the 1971 period should strictly speaking have black trim. These beige seats with head-rests are in fact likely to be from a much later Midget 1500.

head-rest fittings. These, however, were as yet only found on some American export cars, and not offered as an option on home market cars before late 1972. There were new door casings to go with the new seats, featuring a pattern of two groups of horizontal lines, and with black plastic door pulls.

The traditional style spring-spoke steering-wheel had given way to a three-spoke alloy wheel, with five round holes drilled in each spoke, and a 'simulated leather-bound rim'. The steering-wheel boss was more prominent and was also finished in simulated something-or-other. The Midget had an MG badge in the centre of the steering-wheel, while the Sprite had a blank steering-wheel boss. A new corporate Austin-Morris stalk switch on the steering-column controlled the indicators, the headlamp flasher and dip switch (good-bye to the foot-operated dip switch), as well as the horn. The headlamp flasher was now standard, as were twin horns.

A minor change on the instrumentation side was that the warning lamp for a dirty oil filter – a short-lived 1960s BMC experiment – had disappeared. The water temperature gauge abandoned all pretensions to accuracy and now carried simple 'Cold – Normal – Hot' markings. There was a new rear-view mirror of the dipping, anti-dazzle type. The windscreen was now of the latest Triplex zone-toughened glass (laminated on North American cars).

There was much less in the way of mechanical change. In fact, the most important alteration was a new exhaust system with a second silencer at the back, mounted rather prominently and clearly visible under the rear bumper. The old metal gear-lever turret – a legacy from Frog-eye days – was replaced by a rubber turret which was covered by an extended vinyl gaiter. Useful additions such as an interior light mounted below the centre of the dashboard, with courtesy door-operated switches, and a boot light were not introduced at the start of the 1970 model year

but as running changes over the next few months. There were also new telescopic stays for the bonnet and boot-lid, while a new type of heater with rather improved output was fitted.

OPTIONS

It is of interest to note that when the new face-lifted Spridgets were launched in October 1969, for the first time they cost the same. The basic price had now been increased to £625, or £818 including Purchase Tax. Car prices in general were now beginning to climb upwards, and regular price increases would become far more common in the 1970s than before. The list of extras was pruned, with several items now being standard. So the only options, in fact, were the wire wheels, tonneau cover, anti-roll bar, oil cooler, hard-top, and radial-ply tyres, with the laminated windscreen disappearing as a home market option in 1970.

Export models could still be supplied with the laminated screen, a cigar lighter, white-wall tyres, a steering-column lock and, if required, a factory-fitted radio. The low compression engine option was discontinued during 1970 (but low-compression engines would shortly re-appear as standard on all North American cars). In the home market, radios were dealer-installed, as were seat-belts and items such as luggage racks, wing mirrors, etc.

FAREWELL TO THE SPRITE

Apart from the face-lifted 1970 models, the Leyland influence would soon make itself felt in a more drastic fashion. Donald Stokes was not a great believer in the value of traditional brand names. Two of the great BMC successes had been the Mini-Cooper and the Austin-Healey. Unfortunately, from an accountant's point of view, both involved paying royalties out of the company's coffers, to John Cooper and Donald Healey respectively. In 1970, the Leyland board decided, on Stokes' recommendation, to terminate these two royalty agreements, and with them, to discontinue both the Mini-Cooper and the sole remaining Austin-Healey model, the Sprite.

Stokes called Donald Healey, who went to the Triumph factory in Coventry to be informed of the decision. If you believe Healey's autobiography, Stokes on this occasion also indicated his intention to discontinue MG, to give Triumph a clear field in the sports car market. According to his own recollection, the reticent and gentlemanly Donald Healey did not have much to say on this occasion,

although he must have been sorely tempted . . .

In truth, the connection between the Healeys and BMC/BLMC had been growing ever more tenuous over the years, especially so after the merger. None of the Healey family's proposals for new Austin-Healey cars had been approved, and the practice of Healey's shops at Warwick being an unofficial adjunct to the BMC motorsports department had also ceased after the Stokes-dictated withdrawal from sports car racing in 1968.

The last Mini-Coopers were made in 1971, and the last Austin-Healey badged Sprite was produced in December 1970. From January 1971, there was a 'new' model in the BLMC range, the Austin Sprite (the A-AN10

For 1971, a return was made to the bright windscreen frame. Except for badges and name-plates, the Sprite was now identical to the Midget. This is the rare Austin Sprite, after the Healey name was dropped.

The dashboard was not changed, and this solid-spoke steering-wheel is most likely from a later Midget 1500 rubber-bumper model. A 1971 car should have a series of holes in each steering-wheel spoke.

Midget engines had the MG sticker on the rocker cover but were otherwise totally identical to Sprite engines. 1971 was the last model year for the green 12C series of engines, and this is yet another variation of the 'BMC Engine Green' colour. Later cars had the black 12V series engines.

The round rear wheelarch came back for the 1972 model year Midgets, but now with a lip above the wheelarch. The roll-over bar is not a standard item, and the dark green colour may be the 1971 Racing Green. This trim colour is Autumn Leaf. This was the first year for the second-type Rostyle wheels, also found on MGBs.

There was no change to the front end of the Midget at this stage . . .

. . . nor to the rear end.

Press Reactions

The Spridget was still capable of making a good impression on road testers. *The Motor* published a final road test of the Sprite (still an Austin-Healey but only just) in the autumn of 1970, and *The Autocar* put a Midget through its paces in early 1971. The sheer fun factor dominated the general view of these cars. The improved equipment with more standard features compared to earlier cars was commended and the steering merited high praise as ever. The handling was described as 'predictable' by *The Motor* and 'excellent' by *The Autocar*, while the ride was found to be 'improved' by *The Motor* and 'firm' by *The Autocar*.

Performance was little affected by the higher gearing. Top speeds were measured around 94–95mph (151–153kph), with acceleration times from 0–60mph (0–100kph) of 13.5 to 14 seconds. The overall fuel consumption during tests was around 30mpg (1,100km/100l) in both cases. Both test cars were fitted with Michelin ZX radial tyres, still an optional extra, and at this time fitted in preference to Dunlop radials.

Criticisms were levelled at the still-unsynchronized first gear, although the change quality was excellent. The layout of the facia with the scattered switch gear was considered dated. The seats were found wanting in lateral support, and the cockpit and driving position were beginning to feel rather cramped. Similarly, the boot space was found limited. The new heater might give a tremendous output but was still of the water-valve type. It was now described as 'crude', since it could only be turned off completely by the under-bonnet tap.

To sum up, while the Spridget might have been developed over the years, in some areas it had by now been overtaken by the improvements introduced elsewhere in the motor industry.

Car magazine published a comparative test of the latest Midget and the Triumph Spitfire (now in Mark IV guise with a revised rear-end design) in June 1971, and found in favour of the Spitfire. Notwithstanding the fact that the Midget cost less and performed better, the 'much more modern' Spitfire had better handling and roadholding. (The Triumph engineers had successfully improved the rear suspension's previously wayward geometry.) The Spitfire also featured a roomier and more comfortable cockpit.

To *Car* magazine, the Midget 'felt outdated' but the Spitfire 'should be good for a few more years yet – especially with the boost of a 1500 engine'. When their wish was granted in 1974, both the arch rivals would receive this particular boost. Most tellingly, however, *Car* magazine's testers all but openly declared their preference for a Ford Escort 1300 GT, even a Mini 1275 GT, over both open two-seaters.

series). Apart from revised badges, it was absolutely identical to the last of the Austin-Healey Sprites.

One of the most renowned sports car names of the post-war period was thus laid to rest with very little ceremony after eighteen successful years. British Leyland did produce revised owner's handbooks and sales brochures carrying the Austin Sprite name. However, to continue production of the Sprite at all was largely a meaningless charade, and as the Sprite had only been sold in the home market since late 1969, the actual figures involved were miniscule. There were only another 1,022 Sprite enthusiasts who availed themselves of the opportunity to purchase one of these Austins before production finally ceased in mid-1971. From now on, it was the MG Midget or nothing.

The actual 1971 models had been very little modified, although a combined steering-column and ignition lock was now fitted as standard on all cars (including home market models) and the horn push was moved back to the centre of the steering-wheel. There were further revisions to the colour range, which was now totally composed of BLVC colours. For the first time in a number of years, there was an alternative trim colour to black. The new colour was a medium tan or brown colour which BL's colour stylists could not resist calling Autumn Leaf. As was the practice with the Spridgets, the carpets matched the remainder of the interior trim. As for the North American export version of the MG Midget, it was now fitted with side-marker lamps and reflectors, and also sported triple windscreen wipers to comply with the new US legislation requiring a larger swept glass area.

UNDERNEATH THE (ROUND) ARCHES . . .

The revised 1972 model of the MG Midget created a little bit of extra interest – and has indeed created its own niche amongst *aficionados* of the Spridgets – for one reason only: it reverted to full, round, rear wheelarches, for the first time since the original Frogeye. British Leyland stylists still missed the

What they did to the round-arch Midget for the American market in 1974. The big rubber overriders were also in evidence on the MGB models. Note triple wipers, head-rests and sidemarker lamps.

Without a reference point to indicate the scale, it can be difficult to judge the size of a Spridget, especially in the side view, so well-proportioned is the overall design. However, the size of the wheels in relation to the car suggests it is quite small! This is particularly noticeable on the round arch model.

By 1973, radial tyres finally became standard, and head-rests were now a much more common factory-fitted optional extra, also on home market cars.

Fashions in car colours change, but for a time in the early 1970s yellow, orange and very bright red were all the rage. At one time, four out of nine Midget colours came from this end of the spectrum: Bronze Yellow, Flame Red, Blaze and Harvest Gold. The black sills were another typical period feature.

Of the later Midgets, the round arch model of the 1972–1974 period is the most sought-after type. This 1973 model is obviously well looked after, and has been fitted with a few useful accessories.

The luggage rack is almost a must, bearing in mind the rather limited boot space on the Spridgets, and certainly gives more scope for a touring holiday – if you are not worried about security! The rear fog-guard lamps would only become a legal requirement on cars registered in or after 1980, and were not originally found on Midgets, except if fitted by dealers on late 1500 models held over in stock.

The matt-black egg-crate grille with its chrome trim and central badge was common to all Midgets of the 1969–1974 period.

opportunity to harmonize the wheelarch design front and rear: the front wheelarches were not changed, but the new rear wheelarches sported a pronounced lip!

The other very obvious modification was the new Rostyle wheel design, which was similar to that found on the MGB since the introduction of Rostyle wheels on this model in 1969. These wheels still featured the combination of silver rim and black centre, but with a pattern of four long and four short silver-painted spokes creating a clover-leaf design. A similar style of wheel was found on certain models of Ford and Vauxhall saloon cars.

Under the bonnet was a slightly modified engine, and the engine number prefix was now changed, in line with the new Austin-Morris coding system. These new prefixes began with 12V. The number 12, as ever, indicated the engine capacity but V now prosaically meant Vertical – which was Austin-Morris shorthand for telling us that this was an in-line engine for a rear-wheel-drive car. This prefix was followed by a three-figure code number which determined the actual specification and application of the engine. The Midget engine-number code then had the letter F for twin carburettors, and finally an H or an L for High or Low compression.

The home market cars still had the 8.8:1 compression ratio, but the low compression ratio of 8.0:1 made a comeback on North American export cars. Although the actual changes to the engines were limited, one very obvious point was that these new engines were always painted black. This was in place of the traditional BMC engine colours of green (most cars, usually including the Spridgets), red (some MGs) or silver grey-green (the Big Healeys and the MGC). Actually, a rather more important change during 1972 was that the dynamo was finally replaced by an alternator. The fuel tank capacity was increased to 7 Imperial gallons (32 litres).

ADJUSTMENTS

A number of adjustments was made to the interior of the new round-arch model. The toggle switches were replaced by flat rocker switches. There was also a big, corporate British Leyland gear lever knob; its size dictated by the requirement to fit an over-drive switch on some models, although that item was always denied the Midget buyer! Also, a new type of non-swivelling door pull appeared, colour-coded to match the trim.

Static seat-belts were now factory-fitted rather than dealer-installed, but were still an extra-cost item. While technically an option, if you really did not want them, you needed to specify this at the time of ordering the car. There was a new trim colour: Black gave way to Navy, a blue so dark that you needed to look twice before you realized that it was not black. This was found on most cars, with Autumn Leaf featuring only on blue or green Midgets. Head-rests (or, as British Leyland was originally ill-advised enough to call them, head *restraints*) were now an officially quoted factory-fitted extra. Better quality carpet was fitted.

The round-arch Midget lasted for three years, and was the last version of the 1,275cc A-series engined Midget Mark III. There was little in the way of change during this period. For the 1973 model year, Autumn Leaf was replaced by the new trim colour Ochre – a yellow-brown, rather muddy-looking colour – with Navy still the alternative. Ochre did not prove terribly popular, and for 1974 there was a return to the well-tried and well-liked trim colours of Black and Autumn Leaf.

During the production period of the round-arch model, a modified steering-wheel with one long slot in each spoke was introduced. On 1973 models, 145-13 radial tyres were finally standardized on home market cars as well as those for North America. The 5.20-13 cross-ply tyres were only fitted to the, by now, very small number of cars destined for other export markets. In fact, if the Abingdon production control statistics are to be believed, production of cars for export markets other than North America ceased completely in 1972, although a small number of cars probably still found their way to other overseas destinations.

NORTH AMERICAN VARIATIONS

The North American export models continued to develop along slightly different lines. For the 1973 model, US brochures still quoted the power output as 62bhp, but no power output was quoted in the 1974 model year brochure. North American cars were now fitted as standard with head-rests, two-speed wipers with electric rather than manual washers, hazard warning lights, a cigar-lighter, a door-mounted exterior mirror on the driver's side, seat-belts, and a lockable glove-box in the padded facia. Whitewall radial-ply tyres were quoted as an option on North American cars.

A whole range of accessories was available to the American Midget buyer. These were mostly made in the USA and supplied by British Leyland Motors Inc for dealer fitment. They included wheel-trim rings, radio, centre console, electric clock, luggage rack (with ski adapters if required), grille guard and rear-bumper guard, a wooden gear-lever knob, rubber floor-mats, and 'a full range of other sports car accessories'.

Also available was a full line of SCCA-approved competition parts, should anyone wish to take a Midget racing. The 1974 North American models were, in addition, fitted with a seat-belt warning light, adjustable rheostat-type panel lights, and the most enormous rubber overriders for the front and rear bumpers – the first step in MG's attempts to meet the new US bumper requirements.

SELLING WELL

The Midget continued to sell reasonably well but not spectacularly. Annual production in the years 1971–1973 was in the order of 14–16,000 cars, with more than 75 per cent being exported to North America. The home market sales had a fillip in 1972. Now that the Sprite had been discontinued, over 4,600 Midgets were built to home market specification in this year, the best-ever annual home market production figure for the Midget. This was despite prices creeping inexorably upwards. In 1972 for the first time, the tax-paid price of the MG Midget crossed the threshold of £1,000, as the car cost exactly £1,003 at the end of the year. By the time the round-arch model was discontinued in October 1974, the list price would be £1,204, now including Car Tax and VAT, which replaced Purchase Tax in 1973.

In the USA, the Midget cost $2,699 in 1973, comfortably the cheapest sports car available; the Spitfire cost $2,895, and the VW Karmann Ghia coupe $2,800. While it would be stretching credibility to consider this Volkswagen as a sports car, its performance was actually quite comparable to that of the Midget, while its comfort, build quality and legendary reliability may well have tipped the scales in its favour as far as many North American purchasers were concerned.

Summing up, the period from 1968 to 1974 saw plenty of changes to the Spridgets, but mostly of a cosmetic nature. In terms of performance or handling, there was very little to choose between the first 1,275cc-engined cars of 1966 and their descendants eight years later. The car was considered to be old-fashioned and out-dated by most contemporary observers, although many forgave the Midget its deficiencies because it was still such fun to drive.

There was, however, a general yearning for British Leyland to produce a new small sports car, replacing both its ageing contenders, Spitfire and Midget. When the mid-

The face-lift for the 1970 model year gave the Midget these large name-plates on the black sill panels, as well as the corporate British Leyland badge just in front of the doors – called variously the 'mangle handle' or the 'plug hole' badge.

The later style rear lights were common also to the MGB, as were the small separate reversing lamps. The locking filler cap was either an optional extra or an after-market accessory.

The external push-button door handles with key-operated locks were originally introduced in 1964. External locks were perhaps a bit pointless on an open sports car!

The Rostyle wheel and rear wheelarch in detail. The chrome trim rings on this car are after-market accessories, although MGs could be supplied with chrome Rostyle wheels. The small MG badge in the wheel centre is a bit of owner's license!

Not all of the later Midgets had a door mirror on the passenger side but it is a useful accessory even on an open car, and this is the original type in the correct position.

The 1969–1974 style grille badge in close-up.

engined Fiat X1/9 appeared at the end of 1972 (although not at first available in Britain or North America), it was obvious that comparisons would be made between this and the small British sports cars, and hardly favourable to the latter. What was Leyland waiting for? Where was the new small MG or Triumph to outshine this Italian interloper?

Austin-Healey Sprite Mark IV and MG Midget Mark III Technical Data

Engine type BMC A-series, four cylinders in-line
Bore and stroke 70.6 × 81.3mm
Capacity 1,275cc
Compression ratio 8.8:1 (optional low compression 8.0:1)
Valves In-line overhead valves operated by pushrods
Carburation Two SU HS2 – 1¼in (32mm)
Maximum power 64bhp (net) at 5,800rpm
Maximum torque 72lb ft at 3,000rpm
Clutch Single dry-plate diaphragm spring 6½in (16.5cm), hydraulically operated
Gearbox Four-speed manual, synchromesh on 2nd, 3rd and top
Gear ratios 1st 3.2:1, 2nd 1.916:1, 3rd 1.357:1, top 1.00:1, reverse 4.120:1
Final drive ratio 4.22:1 (to October 1968); 3.909:1 (from October 1968)
Suspension:
    Front: Independent with wishbones and coil springs, lever arm shock absorbers, anti-roll bar optional.
    Rear: Live axle with semi-elliptic rear springs, lever arm shock absorbers.
Brakes:
    Front: 8¼in (21cm) discs
    Rear: 7in (18cm) drums
Steering Rack-and-pinion
Wheels 3.5 × 13 disc (to 1969), 4½J × 13 Rostyle (from 1969), 4J × 13 wire optional
Tyres 5.20-13 cross-ply; 145-13 radial ply optional (1968 onwards)
Wheelbase 80in (2.03m)
Track:
    Front: 1966–1969: 46⁵⁄₁₆in (1.17m); 1969–1974 with Rostyle wheels, 46⁹⁄₁₆in (1.18m)
    Rear: 1966–1969 disc: 44¾in (1.14m); wire: 45¼in (1.15m)
        1969–1974: with Rostyle wheels, 45in (1.14m)
Overall length 137⅜in (3.49m)
Overall width 54⅞in (1.39m) – disc wheels; 56½in (1.43m) wire wheels
Overall height (hood up) 48⅝in (1.23m)
Ground clearance 5in (127mm)
Fuel tank capacity 6 Imperial gallons (27 litres) to 1972; 7 Imperial gallons (32 litres) from 1972
Weights:
    Kerbside weight: 1966–1969: 1,575lb (714kg)
                  1969–1974: 1,632lb (740kg)
    Gross vehicle weight: 1966–1969: 1,925lb (873kg)
                  1969–1974: 2,129lb (966kg)

PERFORMANCE:
Top speed 94mph (150kph) – 96mph (155kph) with 3.909 rear axle
0–60mph (0–100kph) 14 seconds
Standing ¼-mile 19 seconds
Fuel consumption 30–36mpg (1,100–1,300km/100l)

7 Triumph, and Tragedy

A new sports car range was pencilled in by Leyland's product planners, but project 'Bullet' (which emerged as the Triumph TR7 in 1975), was never intended as a Midget/Spitfire replacement. Instead, it was scheduled to replace the Triumph TR6 and the MGB, although continued demand from North America forced British Leyland to keep the MGB in production for another five years. The dramatic wedge shape of the TR7, and the fact that it was for a long time available only as a fixed-head coupe, made it a controversial car from the start.

In the early 1970s it was widely expected that open cars would eventually become outlawed in America, and this gloomy forecast was instrumental in Leyland's development of the TR7 as a closed car. In many other respects, the design features of the TR7 were based on market research and information relayed back from Leyland's North American sports car dealers. It was highly ironical, therefore, that a car which was so deliberately designed with this one market in mind, should end up being outsold by the MGB in the American market.

The TR7 was intended to spawn a whole range of sports cars. There was the potentially exciting TR7 Sprint, with the Dolomite Sprint sixteen-valve engine. This saw limited production but was for all practical purposes replaced by the Rover V8-engined TR8, which was sold in some numbers in North America but which was aborted just before the intended launch in the home market.

Then, there were the long-wheelbase versions of the TR7 (fitted also with the V8 engine) which became the fastback 2 + 2 Lynx, a potential Triumph Stag replace-ment. When the Lynx was dropped, a last effort was made to keep a TR7-derived car alive. This was project Broadside, an open 2 + 2 or a fastback coupe, fitted with either the V8 or the new 2-litre O-series single overhead camshaft engine.

BLEAK PROSPECTS

Conspicuously absent was a smaller, less expensive sports car, bearing either the MG or the Triumph badge. In truth the faltering fortunes of British Leyland in the years 1973–1977 meant that there was simply no money to spend on sports car development, apart from what was being absorbed by the TR7 and its derivatives. British Leyland at this time still considered itself as a large-scale manufacturer of family cars, an image that was echoed by the Ryder report commissioned by the government in 1974, and which led to the effective nationalization of British Leyland in 1975.

The company saw the new Rover SD1 as a much more important project, and development was also going ahead of a smaller version, the SD2 which was supposed to be a Triumph-badged replacement for the Dolomite. The Austin-Morris saloon range was at that time reasonably up-to-date, with the uninspired Marina selling well. The Princess, meanwhile, had just been launched to a generally good reception, and some hopes were still being entertained for the Allegro. The next big project was the Mini replacement, which eventually ended up as the Metro, launched in 1980.

The future looked bleak as far as small sports cars were concerned, and no one in the

Although the Spridgets from 1961 to 1974 no longer had the 'happy smiling face' of the Frog-eye, they still managed to look very cheerful and spritely from the front!

Allowing for slight variations in the type of lights depending on local market requirements, most Spridgets had straight-forward sealed beam headlamps, and these combined sidelights and indicators with a part-white, part-orange lens.

The faithful BMC A-series was still found under the bonnet of the 1973 models but was now painted black. This new engine colour was probably introduced with the 12V series of engine in 1971.

The Navy trim colour was only used in 1972 and 1973. The door casings are the type introduced in 1969 but now with a new type of corporate British Leyland door pull. The Midget even had an ash tray as standard by now.

The heat-formed vinyl seats are of the type common to all cars from 1969 to 1979 and the seat pattern can be clearly seen in this photograph.

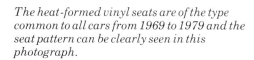

The flat rocker type switches were new in 1971, but the interior light had been there since 1970. The carpet quality was improved for 1972, and it is easier to see here that the trim colour is actually dark blue and not black.

company could any longer seriously nurture any plans, dreams or hopes for an all-new Midget. Leyland was prepared to continue making Midgets and Spitfires for as long as demand existed, but with the absolute minimum of changes, and next to no money being spent on their further development. However, if the company was to continue to sell these models in North America, they had to be prepared to keep them abreast of new safety and emissions legislation which was being introduced in the USA.

EXPORT CONSIDERATIONS

In the States, to confuse the issue further, there were now two sets of different requirements to cope with:

1. The State of California implementing its own emissions standards.
2. The Federal standards which applied in the other forty-nine states.

California State emissions standards were more stringent and usually two to three years ahead of Federal standards. Canadian requirements were not so severe, which explains why British Leyland was able to continue to sell for instance the Mini in Canada, years after it had been withdrawn from the US market.

In 1973, Triumph had begun to fit North American specification Spitfires with a 1,493cc engine. Basically of the same design as the existing Spitfire 1300 engine, and with a lineage going back to the 1953 Standard Eight 803cc engine, this was a specially modified version of the engine then fitted in the Triumph 1500 TC saloon – as well as in certain versions of the Triumph Toledo. The extra capacity enabled Triumph to de-tune the engine and fit all the extra plumbing required by US emissions control laws, and still keep a reasonable performance.

As far as the A-series engine was concerned, there was no real possibility of stretching it any further than the existing 1,275cc capacity. There did not seem a great deal of point in taking another Austin-Morris engine, such as the 1,500cc E-series from the Maxi and Allegro models, and go through the re-design required to comply with American statutes. So, the decision was made to adapt the Spitfire 1500 engine to fit into the Midget.

Bumper Impact

The other important factor looming up was the new American bumper impact legislation, which required bumpers to be able to withstand a 5mph (10kph) collision. The initial response to the proposed legislation had been the hideous overriders found on the 1974 North American model MG Midget and MGB, but these were only a stop-gap. The only solution was to develop all-new impact-absorbing bumper designs, and because these required modifications to the basic bodyshell, it was decided to fit the new bumpers to the Midget and the MGB in all markets.

Unfortunately, someone made a trifling error in translating the bumper height requirements, and at the last moment it became necessary to raise the ride height by 1in (25mm). This would drastically alter the Midget's handling although to compensate, British Leyland at long last fitted the front anti-roll bar as standard.

The actual construction of the bumpers comprised a solid steel bar, covered in energy-absorbing polyurethane foam and finished with a black outer covering of polycarbonate or nylon. Owners had quite a job to keep them clean and shiny; some people resorted to boot polish, but most simply left them to go dull! The depth of the bumpers was greatly increased and the new front bumper included a narrow, slit-like air-intake in place of the traditional radiator grille.

The front indicators were located in the actual bumper – now with all-amber lenses, as the sidelights were incorporated in the headlamps. At the rear of the car, the number-plate was put below the bumper on home market cars, but the narrower American number-plate could be accommodated between the reversing lamps. Export models therefore had the number-plate bracket above the bumper. Two rear number-plate lamps were fitted on all cars.

Back to Square Arches

One important modification was made to the bodywork. The round-arch rear wings had proved to weaken the structure of the rear-end, so the new model returned to the square arches of the 1961–1971 pattern. Not that there was any risk of structural failure on the round-arch cars; it was merely that the square-arch rear wings with the deeper area of metal above the arch made a greater contribution to the overall strength of the rear-end of the car. This, of course, helped to meet the American requirements.

Unfortunately, the bodywork modifications and new bumpers pushed the weight of the car up by about 1½cwt (76kg). Thus, as far as home market cars were concerned, the

The Midget 1500 was originally offered with wire wheels, now with octagonal nuts. The rubber bumpers did little for the car's looks.

*Pre- and post-Leyland Midgets together, highlighting the differences in
radiator grille, bumper, chrome trim and badging.*

If you have set your heart on a chrome-bumper Spridget there is, despite the cosmetic alterations, not a great deal of difference between a 1970s car (in the foreground) or a 1960s model (at the back). Your choice between such cars, even with ten years' difference in age, should be governed by condition, price and, of course, availability.

'Even Midgets have feelings . . .' This delightfully set shot of two friendly Midgets evokes a rather more recent advertisement for the Mini.

bigger engine was required to keep up the performance of the car. In the state of tuning used in the Midget, the Spitfire 1500 engine gave 65bhp (now measured by the DIN method) at 5,500rpm, and torque was 77lb ft at 3,000rpm. As it turned out, the Midget 1500 performed rather better than any previous Spridget had done, with a true top speed of just over 100mph (160kph), and a 0–60mph (0–100kph) acceleration time of just over 12 seconds.

Alas, it was a different story as far as North American specification cars were concerned. Instead of twin SUs, they had a single Zenith-Stromberg carburettor, and the compression ratio was down from 9:1 to 7.5:1. The American specification engine yielded a reluctant 50bhp at 5,000rpm, with torque down to 67lb ft at 2,500rpm. It took more than 14 seconds to get to 60mph (100kph), and the car ran out of steam around 85mph (140kph).

MIDGET 1500

The new rubber-bumpered Midget 1500 model, together with similarly-equipped MGB models, greeted MG enthusiasts visiting the corporate British Leyland stand in the Earls Court Motor Show in October 1974. The bumpers undoubtedly made the biggest

From the rear, the rubber bumper was also much in evidence.

MG Midget 1500 Technical Data

Engine type Triumph Spitfire, four cylinders in-line
Bore and stroke 73.7×87.5mm
Capacity 1,493cc
Compression ratio 9.0:1, North America: 7.5:1
Valves In-line overhead valves operated by pushrods
Carburation Two SU HS4 – 1½in (38mm) – North America: One Zenith–Stromberg
Maximum power 65bhp DIN/5,500rpm; North America: 50bhp DIN/5,000rpm
Maximum torque 77lb ft/3,000rpm; North America: 67lb ft/2,500rpm
Clutch Single dry-plate diaphragm spring 7¼in (18cm), hydraulically operated
Gearbox Four-speed manual, synchromesh on all forward gears
Gear ratios 1st 3.41:1, 2nd 2.11:1, 3rd 1.43:1, top 1.00:1, reverse 3.75:1
Final drive ratio 3.909:1 (1974–1977); 3.72:1 (1977–1979)
Suspension:
    Front: Independent with wishbones and coil springs, lever arm shock absorbers, anti-roll bar;
           North America: anti-roll bar 1977–1979
    Rear: Live axle with semi-elliptic rear springs, lever arm shock absorbers
Brakes:
    Front: 8¼in (21cm) discs
    Rear: 7in (18cm) drums. Dual circuits on home market cars from 1978
Steering Rack-and-pinion
Wheels $4.5J \times 13$ Rostyle wheels; $4J \times 13$ wire wheels optional
Tyres 145-13 radial ply
Wheelbase 80in (2.03m)
Track:
    Front: Rostyle 46⁹⁄₁₆in (1.18m); wire wheels: 46⁵⁄₁₆in (1.17m)
    Rear: Rostyle 45in (1.14m); wire wheels 45¼in (1.15m)
Overall length 141in (3.58m)
Overall width Rostyle: 54⅞in (1.39m); wire wheels: 56½in (1.43m)
Overall height (hood up) 48¼in (1.22m)
Ground clearance 3¼in (83mm)
Fuel tank capacity 7 Imperial gallons (32 litres); North America: 6½ Imperial gallons (29.5 litres)
Weights:
    Kerbside weight: 1,774lb (805kg); North America: 1,849lb (839kg)
    Gross vehicle weight: 2,154lb (977kg); North America: 2,229lb (1,011kg)

PERFORMANCE:
Top speed 100mph (160kph); North America: 85mph (137kph)
0–60mph (0–100kph) 12 seconds; North America: 14 seconds
Standing ¼-mile 18.5 seconds; North America: 20 seconds
Fuel consumption 30–35mpg (1,100–1,200km/100l)

impact on most observers. That a Triumph Spitfire engine was now fitted under the bonnet was not relished by the majority of MG enthusiasts.

While the improved performance of the car made a favourable impression, the handling had deteriorated markedly, as was soon pointed out in independent road tests. The car had become very throttle-sensitive and was far more apt to oversteer.

Among the other changes to the Midget 1500 was a new, lower-geared steering-rack – another Triumph component, actually – but the steering was still relatively high-

By contrast to the cheerful aspect of the Frog-eye and the chrome-bumper Spridgets, the rubber-bumper model looks a bit down in the mouth; not surprisingly in view of the fact that it had had to swallow a Triumph engine!

The bumper tends to dominate also the rear view of the car. Note the location of the rear number-plate on this home-market model.

Some people prefer the rubber-bumper cars in dark colours where you 'lose' the bumpers, but this combination of Inca Yellow and black is certainly quite effective.

The Rostyle wheels were more typical of the Midget 1500. This 1979 car was made towards the end of Midget production.

geared at less than three turns from lock to lock, and was one of the car's best features. There was also a new gearbox, finally with a synchronized first gear, but unfortunately, the Morris Marina single-rail gearbox was used. Originally derived from the Triumph Herald gearbox, it had rather more widely spaced ratios than hitherto found on the Midget and the shift quality was not so nice as on the old BMC gearbox. The clutch had been increased in size to 7¼in. Another small change was that the Midget reverted to a mechanical fuel pump.

Equipment and Interior Details

The new model did rather better in the equipment stakes. Twin door mirrors became standard, and hazard-warning lamps were introduced on the home market cars. The tonneau cover was now supplied as standard. The only extras quoted in 1974 were wire wheels, head restraints and the hard-top. However, by 1976 the wire-wheel option had been discontinued on home market cars (they remained available on cars supplied in North America to the end of production), and the

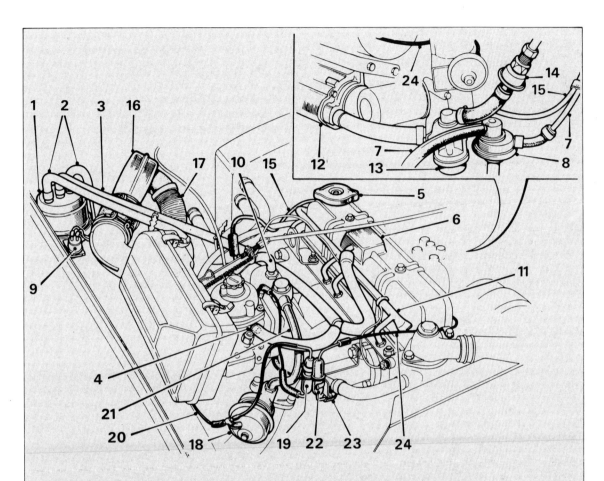

Typical underbonnet layout of the late model North American specification MG Midget 1500 (1976 model shown).

THE EMISSION CONTROL COMPONENTS

1	Charcoal absorption canister	13	Diverter valve
2	Vapour lines	14	Check valve
3	Purge line	15	Diverter valve pipe
4	Restricted connection	16	Air temperature control valve
5	Sealed oil filler cap	17	Hot air hose
6	Oil separator/flame trap (arrester)	18	Exhaust gas/re-circulation valve
7	Fuel pipe	19	EGR valve flame trap
8	Fuel pump	20	EGR valve line to carburettor choke cam
9	Running-on control valve	21	EGR valve pipe
10	Running-on control pipe	22	Distributor flame trap
11	Air manifold	23	Distributor flame trap line to carburettor
12	Air pump	24	Flame trap line distributor vacuum unit

hard-top was discontinued at around the same time. On the other hand, the head-rests became a standard fitting in early 1977. If radio was ordered to be installed by the dealer, a centre console with a speaker could now be supplied, and this console became standard equipment, together with an aerial, in 1978. The console then also incorporated a cigar lighter.

There were few differences in the interior, but an immediate recognition point was that the Midget 1500's steering-wheel had solid spokes. The background colour of the MG badge on the steering-wheel boss was changed from red to gold on the 1976 models. As one American market brochure memorably put it, 'The Golden Octagon symbolizes

more than 50 years of sports car leadership'. A year later, the badge was changed to silver letters and octagon on a black background. Also in 1977, the static seat-belts were replaced by the inertia reel type.

The initial run of the rubber-bumper cars featured the same colour range as the superseded model, but some new colours were introduced in early 1975, and the policy of annual colour revisions was continued. The trim colours of Black and Autumn Leaf were continued until 1977, but for the 1978 model year Autumn Leaf was replaced by a new Beige trim colour. There was no change to the seat design or style, unlike the MGB which acquired deck-chair striped nylon upholstery for the home market models in 1976.

There was little change to the interior, although the centre console found on the later cars may be seen here. This is another non-original steering-wheel.

Note that the carburettors have now changed side, as has the trunking for the
heater air-intake. On this engine, the Triumph origins have been camouflaged
by a non-standard rocker cover.

There were a few more changes on the 1978
model year cars. The passenger-door mirror
was deleted from the specification, leaving
only the outside mirror on the driver's side –
perhaps someone decided that Midget owners
never took their cars across the Channel. The
rear axle ratio was raised from 3.9:1 to 3.72:1.
The stylized MG wing badge was removed
from the facia – this was penny-pinching if
anything ever was. The instruments on home
market cars were replaced with Triumph
Spitfire instruments, which meant that the
Midget lost its oil pressure gauge, and the
speedometer and rev counter changed places.

North American export cars had their instruments commonalized with the North
American MGB. During 1978, two-speed
wipers and a handbrake warning light were
added to the specification. Virtually the only
modification made on the 1979 models was
the introduction, at long last, on home mar-

ket cars of a dual-circuit braking system
some eleven years after this had first been
fitted to North American export models!

GOODBYE TO THE MIDGET

Midget production finally came to an end in
November 1979. The last 500 home market
cars were all finished in Black although,
unlike the last home market MGB cars a year
later, they were not advertised as a 'Limited
Edition'. This final batch of Midgets were
also supplied with a commemorative plaque
for the dashboard, bearing the inscription
'1929–1979 – Fifty years of the MG Midget'.

Around the time the car went out of production, new legislation was being introduced in the UK to make rear fog-guard
lamps mandatory. Although no Midget ever

left the Abingdon factory so equipped, dealers were advised by circular letter to ensure that cars held in stock were retro-fitted with rear fog-guard lamps if they were not registered before the new law came into force. As a matter of fact, many Midgets only went on the road well in 1980 or even 1981; towards the end, home market sales had slowed considerably. Not with a bang but a whimper . . .

NORTH AMERICAN TWILIGHT

If Leyland's main reason for producing the Midget 1500 at all had been their wish to continue to sell the car in North America, they must have been sadly disappointed by the reception given to the new model by American magazines. *Road & Track* asked bluntly, 'Why would anyone want one?', and *Car and Driver* called it trash. On the other hand they advised, 'Maybe you'd better get one while they last'. The American specification Midget 1500 was slow, it handled worse than the home market model (the anti-roll bar was only fitted as standard to American-specification models in 1977), and although 'small' might equal 'cute' in North America, the cockpit seemed even more cramped and uncomfortable to the average American than to the average Brit.

The Midget 1500 was at first not available in California. During 1975, however, the engine was developed to accept unleaded petrol and the exhaust system was fitted with a catalytic converter, which once again made the Midget acceptable under the special Californian emissions standards. Eventually, the lead-free tolerant engine and the catalyst were fitted to all North American specification cars. For 1978, North American Midgets adopted the four-spoke safety steering-wheel found on the MGB by this time. Other features introduced on the American-specification cars were an automatic choke, and a steering-column mounted stalk controlling two-speed wipers and an electric windscreen washer.

Local Options

The options available to American Midget purchasers were, as ever, slightly different from those offered in the home market. Wire wheels remained available in North America until the end of production, and so did whitewall tyres. The tonneau cover was quoted as an option, even after it had become standard on UK cars. There was a choice of radios, now including an AM/FM receiver. The wheel-trim rings, rubber floor mats, wooden gear-lever knob and luggage rack all remained available to US or Canadian buyers, and door-edge guards were introduced. British Leyland Motors Inc optimistically continued to quote unspecified 'Optional Competition Equipment' in their US/Canadian market brochures, but there is little evidence that many North American Midget 1500 buyers availed themselves of the opportunity to race their cars in the Sports Car Club of America (SCCA) race series.

As in the home market, the price in the USA had gradually edged up, and the Midget 1500 ended up costing over $5,000 by the time production ended in 1979. This still made it the cheapest sports car on the market; the MGB cost another $1,000, and the Midget's competitors such as the Spitfire and the Fiat X1/9 were more expensive too. One senses the despair of the old-school American sports car enthusiasts who had been weaned on MGs twenty or thirty years before.

The MGB still retained much of its appeal, but the Midget was too out of date. The news that British Leyland intended to stop production of the Midget was, if anything, greeted almost with relief by American motoring writers, who had to pad out their Midget road test reports with much nostalgia about MG Midgets as they used to be! Of course, this did not prevent the Midget from continuing to sell well in North America, where – as before

— 75 per cent of Midgets continued to find buyers.

OH DEATH, WHERE IS THY STING?

The end was long in coming, but the writing had been on the wall ever since BMC and Leyland merged in 1968. There is little doubt that the original BLMC and British Leyland management headed by Donald Stokes was pre-disposed in favour of Triumph (rather than MG) as the corporation's sports car make. In consequence, future plans were laid which included new Triumphs, but the gradual discontinuation of the MG range and the idea of closing the Abingdon factory had been promoted several times from different quarters within the company. One suggestion was that MG final assembly might simply be moved to the body plant at Swindon, where both Midget and MGB bodies were produced.

However, the Ryder report still saw a future for British Leyland as a true large-scale manufacturer. After nationalization in 1975, Alex Park became the company's chief executive. A charming and gentlemanly Yorkshireman, Alex Park was charged by the Labour government with implementing the Ryder plan. Apart from anything else, he was hamstrung by the political impossibility of making any reductions in the Leyland workforce, or of closing any of the too-many factories. It took two years to realize that the Ryder plan was an impossibility and that drastic remedies were required if British Leyland was to survive at all.

THE EDWARDES FACTOR

Then in 1977, South African-born Michael Edwardes (then an executive of Chloride who had served on the government-sponsored National Enterprise Board) was asked to take over as chief executive of British Leyland. Having acquired a degree of familiarity with Leyland's many problems through his work on the NEB, Edwardes was at first hesitant. He eventually agreed to take over from 1 November 1977. Alex Park gracefully stepped aside and resigned from the Leyland board within a few weeks.

Unlike previous British Leyland top managers, who had to some extent tried to bury everything under the corporate name and logo, Edwardes was inclined to bring back the old and still honoured marque names, allowing separate identities to flourish once again. An early decision was to split the Leyland Cars conglomerate – responsible for everything from Minis to Daimler limousines – into two new groups:

1. Austin Morris for the mass-production family cars.
2. A Jaguar Rover Triumph (JRT) group for the more specialized types of car.

Despite MG's historical ties with Morris and BMC, MG was lumped in with the other specialist makes in JRT, whose title prompted one American observer to quip, 'Whatever happened to MG?'

JRT, as it turned out, would not be a long-lasting edifice. Jaguar was eventually separated out on its own, while Rover, Triumph and the remains of MG were re-integrated in a 'small-medium cars division'. This, under Harold Musgrove's guidance, eventually assumed the name of the Austin Rover Group and later, with the re-incorporation of Land Rover Limited, became the Rover Group we know today.

However, this only happened well after Abingdon had gone, and the original MG sports cars with it. Michael Edwardes arrived at a time when the company was already fully committed to the TR7, by then two years into production. One of his early decisions was to stop work on further derivatives of this car, notably the Lynx. During Edwardes'

Sir Michael Edwardes (born 1930)

Of diminutive stature but large personality, Sir Michael Edwardes was bound to make an impact on the world somewhere somehow. It was rather by coincidence that it happened to be BL.

Edwardes was born in South Africa and came to England as a management trainee with the Chloride battery company in 1951. Yet, after forty years, he still retains his characteristic native accent.

In 1969 he became a member of the Chloride board; soon after he was made chief executive and then executive chairman. He has described himself as a professional manager rather than a capitalist, which is essentially correct. He is above all a businessman, with his sympathies firmly in the private sector. In short, he seems to have been a surprising choice as head of a nationalized company under a Labour government.

In 1975, Sir Don Ryder (later Lord Ryder) asked Michael Edwardes to join the National Enterprise Board (NEB). The NEB under Lord Ryder became the governmental instrument for overseeing the nationalized British Leyland company. Lord Ryder resigned in 1977 and soon after, Leyland's then non-executive chairman, Sir Richard Dobson, was forced to resign.

Michael Edwardes agreed to take over, provided he was given full executive powers. An initial three-year secondment was later extended, and Sir Michael (who was knighted during this period) spent a total of five years as the head of BL.

In his own memoirs of these years, *Back from the Brink*, Sir Michael states that:

The decision to stop MG sports car production created more public fuss and misunderstanding than anything in the whole five years . . . This was perhaps the only occasion on which the Board's commercial judgement was seriously challenged . . . The moral of the episode is clear: you mess around with famous marque names that are loved and cherished by motor enthusiasts at your peril!

However much of a public outcry there was at the time, there is little doubt that the decision of Sir Michael and his board was the right one. And the fate of Abingdon and the MG sports car was only one of the problems that he had to tackle.

During Sir Michael's tenure, old marque loyalties such as Austin, Rover and Jaguar were re-kindled. The co-operative programme with Honda was begun. BL launched the Metro and made good progress on the design of other new models. Many of the smaller subsidiaries were sold, and the decks generally cleared as a first step towards privatization – which had become the firm goal after Margaret Thatcher and the Conservative party came to power in 1979.

When Sir Michael left, he had laid a sound foundation for the modern Rover Group. The now privatized and successful company is his best monument.

tenure of the company, which he renamed BL, the overriding priority became to get the Metro into production, and to follow this up by new medium-sized family cars. Also, Edwardes finally got the government to agree to reduce the size of BL. The first factory to be closed was the TR7 assembly plant at Speke near Liverpool. This was followed in fairly rapid order by the Triumph assembly plant at Canley in Coventry, the Rover SD1 assembly plant at Solihull, and by the MG factory at Abingdon.

THE END OF ABINGDON

Admittedly, the MG factory was ready for euthanasia. Long starved of investment, still even without a mechanized moving assembly line, Abingdon could not have taken on the assembly of a new model without a very major revamp. It was tactless, however, to announce the intention of closing the factory in the week after MG and Abingdon had celebrated their 50th anniversary together in September 1979. Similarly, the excuse that BL lost money on every single MG sports car sold in the USA was ill-chosen when the annual balance sheet showed the company to loose a great deal of tax-payer's money on every vehicle they sold.

There were protests and demonstrations, there were promises of support from MG enthusiasts at home and abroad, and a well-publicized take-over bid from the unlikely source of Aston Martin. All to no avail. The Midget was discontinued first, in November 1979, the last MGB followed in October 1980, and in the following months the plant was run down, eventually to be put up for sale.

However much the sentimentalists, the traditionalists and the nostalgia-seekers might bemoan the loss of Abingdon and of the old-style MG sports car, we cannot doubt that there *was* solid commercial sense behind these difficult decisions. The real tragedy was that no one at BMC, BLMC, British Leyland or BL ever made serious plans for an unbroken continuation of the MG sports car pedigree, after the always inevitable demise of the MG Midget and the MGB.

Austin Rover's decision to keep the proud octagonal badge alive on a line of worthy sporting saloons during the 1980s was honourable enough. With a change of direction after the arrival of Graham Day as chairman of the Rover Group in 1986, we cannot doubt that some day, there will be a revival of the MG sports car, although at the time of writing, we were still waiting! But how easily it could have turned out in an altogether different way, if only . . . Sadly, no survey of MG history in the final two decades of the original company (from 1960 to 1980) is complete without a review of the varied and interesting projects undertaken with a view to replacing those increasingly ancient warriors, the Midget and the MGB. The following chapter is a study, however incomplete and faltering, of those that did not make it.

8 Projects and Promises

Ironically, ideas for alternative small sports cars were being considered within BMC almost from the time the first Frog-eye Sprite was launched in 1958. The catalyst proved to be project ADO15, better known since its launch in August 1959 as the Mini. Even during the gestation period of the Mini, there were those engineers and designers within BMC who saw the small front-wheel drive car as a potential basis for a sports model.

Let it be said however, that the Mini's designer, Alec Issigonis, was not at all interested in sports cars. Indeed, from his early days in the drawing office of Morris Motors at Cowley, he was apt to sneer at any sports car project he might see on a colleague's drawing board. So, any development of Mini-based sports cars had to be undertaken, if not exactly as a cloak-and-dagger operation, at least away from the immediate vicinity of Issigonis' experimental department at Longbridge where the Mini (and subsequently the 1100 and 1800 models) were taking shape.

ACCURATE GUESSWORK

A remarkably prescient article, written by one Bob Cumberford, appeared in the American magazine *Sports Car Illustrated* for June 1960. Cumberford referred to 'recent information from England' and it is very hard not to imagine that he had some sort of inside information about what was going on at Longbridge or Abingdon. Cumberford described and illustrated what he thought might be the new MG Midget, based on the Mini. His drawings show an uncanny resemblance to a car which, possibly around that exact time, was being put together at Longbridge.

This one-off prototype was based on a very early production Austin Seven (Mini), in fact, the second such car to be built. It featured the standard Mini front-end, windscreen and doors, but there was a completely new rear end and obviously the roof was removed altogether. There was sufficient room for occasional seats in the rear of the lengthy cockpit, the tail was rounded with a deep tonneau panel and a fairly small boot-lid which opened downwards in typical Mini fashion, and looked as if it might only have been intended as an access panel to the spare wheel. There was a suggestion of rear wings, finished off with standard Mini tail-lamp units.

It is now difficult to say how seriously this project was taken at Longbridge at the time, but the fact remains that the car was built, whether it was intended merely as a Mini convertible or as a proper sports car. It is even more interesting to realize that this particular car is still in existence. It was sold by BMC around 1962, and has now for more than twenty years been in private ownership in the same family in Cornwall. Apart from the undoubted significance of this car as a prototype, it is also the oldest Mini which is known to exist.

Bob Cumberford's drawings showed an altogether prettier little car. His stylistic imagination, unfettered by boring reality, allowed him to lower the bonnet – always a difficult feat with BMC's gearbox-in-the-sump transverse engines – and push the windscreen backwards. The screen was well raked and lower than the standard Mini windscreen. His sketched-out idea was for a proper two-seater sports car, the rear-end reminiscent of the Frog-eye, with no external boot-lid being apparent, and tail lights of the

Sprite or MGA type. The radiator grille was remarkably similar to the grille which appeared on the MG 1100 in 1962, but was, of course, a fairly obvious development of the MGA grille.

THE MINI SPORTS CAR PROJECT

While Bob Cumberford delved and Longbridge span, Syd Enever's design department at Abingdon had also got their teeth into the Mini sports car project. Their proposal, which was constructed in mock-up form in 1959, was clearly influenced by the forthcoming Sprite/Midget and MGB models. The front-end strongly resembled the MGB, with a similar radiator grille and the typical recessed headlamps (allegedly inspired by the Renault Floride).

The front overhang was very short, which made the proportions of the car in side view slightly awkward. The windscreen and cockpit were moved backwards compared to the Mini, and the intention seems to have been to provide a removable panel in the tonneau to allow for occasional rear seating. The rear-end was very much like the MGB or the Spridget, with vertical tail lights in modest fins, and an external boot-lid. The car looked particularly neat in the rear three-quarter view. One curious feature was that, like the 1961 Spridget, this car had a round front wheelarch and a squared-off rear wheelarch.

This Abingdon project seems to have been given serious consideration by BMC, and was allocated the official project number of ADO34. Alec Issigonis was against the idea, and described it to the MG historian Wilson McComb as: 'A dreadful thing; you just think it's good because it was designed at Abingdon.' Officially, this original ADO34 project was abandoned, much to the disappointment of Syd Enever and everyone at Abingdon, because it would be too expensive to tool up for a new sports car body – presumably the

company had already committed to the 1961 Spridget at this time. Instead, BMC decided to go ahead with the Cooper-tuned derivative of the Mini saloon, launched in 1961 as the Mini-Cooper.

However, ADO34 was not quite defunct. While Abingdon's original proposal was shelved, the idea for a Mini-based sports car lived on and, subsequently, the designers at Longbridge had a go. The later Longbridge project still retained the ADO34 code, but there were spin-offs in the form of an ADO35 coupe version, and an ADO36 Austin-Healey (Sprite) model. There were Longbridge-built styling mock-ups of MG-badged coupes as early as 1960, looking rather like lowered and more sporting versions of the Austin A40 Farina, and it is in fact difficult to say whether this proposal was based on the A40 or on the Mini.

THE FARINA-BUILT PROTOTYPE

By 1963–1964, however, the final version of the Mini-based MG sports car was coming together. This car had a body styled and built by Pininfarina in Italy, looking very much like a smaller version of the Peugeot 204 Convertible from the same designer's pen. It was based on the subframes, mechanical components and engine from a Mini-Cooper 'S' 1,275cc. The unitary body derived strength from a massive central tunnel, and the boot-lid was kept quite small, with a fixed vertical tail panel.

The Farina-built prototype was finished to a very high standard, with interior trim on a rather more luxurious level than was usual on Spridgets, including leather-upholstered seats with adjustable backs. Only the instrument layout looked a bit unfinished, with a Cooper-style three-instrument nacelle straddling the steering-column, and an after-thought of a rev counter sitting on the full-width parcel shelf. With only a few modi-

fications, this car could have gone into production by the mid-to-late 1960s. One imagines that BMC were concerned about the return on a sizeable investment in tooling, bearing in mind that the important American market may not have been ready for a front-wheel-drive sports car. It is also an open question whether the car could have been adapted to the new US legislative requirements coming into force in 1968.

DIVIDED RESPONSIBILITY

While work continued on a front-wheel-drive small sports car at Longbridge, Abingdon was asked to look at the possibility of developing a new conventional sports car with a front engine and rear-wheel drive. The Healey company, meanwhile, was asked to produce a study for a mid-engined sports car – their last official design undertaking for BMC, and quite an advanced project for the early 1960s.

That these two alternative projects were commissioned proves that BMC were intending to remain in the sports car market in the long term. It also proves that they were prepared to examine every possible avenue of future sports car design, presumably with the intention of selecting the one of the three proposals (front-wheel drive, conventional or mid-engined) which seemed to offer the best prospects for the future, depending on the state of the sports car market as it developed in the late 1960s.

EX.234

The Abingdon project, which was given the typical MG-style project number EX.234,

(Left) Three generations of Spridgets lined up, from Frog-eye to rubber bumper model – the difficulty was always in devising a suitable replacement for these cars.

Survivors

Luckily, the Farina-built ADO34 prototype still exists, now cared for by the Rover Group Heritage Trust, and is kept in running order. It was only registered for the road for the first time in 1990, when it took part in the Regency Run for MG cars from London to Brighton, driven by the author.

As far as the derivatives of ADO34 are concerned, a very exciting discovery was made in a Midlands back garden in 1989. This was a completely stripped bodyshell of what appears to be the ADO35 coupe. While there are some significant differences between this body and the photographs taken at Longbridge at the time of the ADO35 coupe, and while the provenance of this particular body remains unknown, it is difficult to imagine what it is if not the remains of ADO35.

This body is now being restored by an enthusiast in East Anglia, and it is likely to end up being fitted with Mini-Cooper 'S' mechanicals. When completed, this car will offer a fascinating glimpse of what might have been, if things had gone slightly different for BMC in the 1960s.

was the last major design undertaken by Syd Enever and the MG design office. Although the most conventional of the three concurrent sports car proposals being studied by BMC, it was not without technical interest. First of all, EX.234 was not quite a replacement for either the Spridget or the MGB. In size it was between the two cars, and was designed to accept either the 1,275cc A-series Spridget engine, or the 1,798cc B-series MGB engine.

Whether this would have been successful in practice is another question. The smaller-engined version would probably have appeared underpowered in comparison, and would not have been a great deal cheaper than the bigger-engined car; but the concept of developing a range of cars with different sizes of engines in the same basic body was novel in 1964.

The other important feature was that EX.234 used the all-independent Hydrolastic suspension, developed by Alex Moulton and produced by Dunlop for the BMC range of front-wheel drive saloons, starting with the 1100 in 1962. Hydrolastic suspension used pressurized fluid as the actual suspension medium, with the front and rear suspension elements interconnected. By the standards of the 1960s, Hydrolastic offered an important advance compared to then-current conventional suspensions, by virtue of offering much-improved levels of comfort without compromising roadholding and handling. Another interesting aspect was that Hydrolastic made separate shock absorbers superfluous, because the system was in effect self-dampening.

Because EX.234 had rear-wheel drive, a special independent rear suspension was developed for the car, with a final-drive unit apparently borrowed from a defunct Austin Gipsy. The Gipsy was the only other rear-wheel drive vehicle with independent rear suspension that BMC had made until then.

EX.234 used an all-new unitary construction body, the styling and construction of which was again entrusted to Pininfarina. The radiator grille, although shallower, and the headlamp recesses gave the car a family resemblance to the MGB. There was a sharply cut-off Kamm-type tail. It was a pretty car, looking not unlike Pininfarina's Alfa Romeo Spider in its later form with cut-off tail. The interior was well fitted out and finished, with an instrument pack probably borrowed from BMC's Riley Kestrel 1100, set in an open parcel shelf. There was an integrated centre console, another unusual feature for the 1960s. The seats were unmistakably Italian, with a rather garish pattern. There was an occasional rear seat but only really suitable for children.

EX.234 seems to have been a very realistic proposal, but would undoubtedly have been more of an MGB than a Spridget replacement. By 1966 or so, however, BMC was probably no longer in a position to be able to afford the investment for tooling-up the new body. If the car had made it into production, it is possible that the suspension would have been reconsidered, with a conventional set-up replacing the Hydrolastic. Fortunately, EX.234 also survives, in Syd Beer's remarkable collection of MGs in Cambridgeshire.

WAEC

The third project undertaken in the 1960s for a new BMC sports car was entrusted to the Healeys who were asked to look into the possibility of producing a mid-engined sports car. Geoffrey Healey was instrumental in this project, with the styling being undertaken by Les Ireland. The car was based on standard BMC components, with a Mini-Cooper 'S' 1,275cc engine installed transversely behind the seats and, like the other contemporary projects, with Hydrolastic suspension. The project was named WAEC, which stood for 'Wheel At Each Corner'.

WAEC was remarkably advanced in its design, curiously suggestive of the Fiat X1/9 which came quite a few years later. Not only did it share the transverse mid-engine design with the Italian car, but its styling was not dissimilar, especially as WAEC featured a permanent roll-over bar. Where the later Fiat had a removable rigid panel, the Healey prototype featured a hood which folded into the roll-over bar. The car featured rack-and-pinion steering borrowed from the BMC 1100, and a new design of Lockheed disc brakes fitted to all four wheels.

According to Geoffrey Healey, the handling was typical of many mid-engined cars, with excellent roadholding up to a point, and the rear-end suddenly breaking away after that. WAEC was turned over to BMC for assessment, and may to some extent have inspired the subsequent ADO21 project (of which more later). The car does not survive. Geoffrey Healey believes that it was finally broken up in the Triumph factory at Canley.

How Sports Car Illustrated *visualized a Mini-based MG Midget in 1960.*

Conceived around the same time, one of BMC's early studies for a small MG coupe, probably based on the mechanical components from the Mini.

WAEC was not the only Healey proposal for updating or replacing the Spridget. Some years before, during the lifetime of the Frog-eye, the Healeys built what was called the Super Sprite, using a Coventry Climax single overhead camshaft 1,100cc engine. The car was based on a Frog-eye floorpan but had a completely re-styled body. The Super Sprite was envisaged as a higher performance, limited production version, selling obviously at a higher price, with an eye to racing – a formula which had worked well for the Healey company with the Austin-Healey 100 'S' in 1955. There were three Super Sprite prototypes, and the project could easily have become reality. However, BMC declined to become involved, as they were unwilling to entertain the idea of using an engine from an outside company.

THE BRITISH LEYLAND PROJECTS

As previously stated, after the merger between BMC and Leyland in 1968, it became increasingly unlikely that there would ever be a straightforward replacement for any of the old BMC sports cars. Commercial reason also dictated that future development of the MG and Triumph sports car ranges went hand in hand. The biggest hope in the early 1970s was Triumph's Bullet project which became the TR7. But there was still some activity within the Austin Morris division of British Leyland with regard to projects for sports – or at least, sporting – cars.

There was the revival, in 1969–1970, of the idea for a Mini-based sports car. A styling proposal was prepared at Longbridge, but to save time and money on building the prototype, the Italian design company Michelotti was asked to undertake the construction of the car. The Longbridge styling designer Robin Owen (now well-known for his paintings of motor racing subjects) drove a Mini 1275 GT out to Italy. He stayed there for the

period of three months or so while the car was being built, and then drove the finished car back to England. Inevitably, the hand-built prototype was heavier than the original 1275 GT had been, and Robin remembers his disappointment in the reduced performance of the car on the return trip.

The Michelotti Mini

This was project ADO70, often referred to as the Michelotti Mini. It looked surprisingly like the abandoned Healey WAEC, with a built-in roll-over bar, but rather than a folding hood, it had two removable roof panels finished in brushed stainless steel. Some of the styling details were slightly extravagant but could easily have been changed. The car was never actually badged as an MG, and might simply have been marketed as a Mini.

Rob Golding in his comprehensive history of the Mini is not in any doubt, however, that ADO70 would effectively have replaced the MG Midget. He believes, as indeed it seems most likely, that the problems of getting the car to meet the US emissions and safety regulations effectively killed the project. In any case, was the world really ready for a front-wheel drive sports car in 1970?

Condor

Of the whole academy of projects which from time to time were conceived by BMC and British Leyland, let us at least be thankful that we were spared ADO68, also known as Condor. Perhaps rather hastily conceived in 1969, this was supposedly British Leyland's riposte to the Ford Capri.

Using the underpinnings of the forthcoming Morris Marina might not have been a totally good idea. If this were not sufficient as a recipe for disaster, consider the choice of engines, supposed to match the Capri line-up: E-series 1,500cc and 1,750cc from Maxi, and possibly the 2,200cc six-cylinder E-

Syd Enever's thoughts for a Mini-based MG sports car showed a clear family resemblance . . .

series, all adapted to rear-wheel drive, with the Triumph Stag V8 on top.

Various styling proposals were made, the most attractive bearing a resemblance to the Bertone-designed Fiat Dino coupe, others resembling lower and more aggressive versions of the Marina coupe. Strictly speaking out of the Spridget league, the Condor might also not have been badged as an MG. In any case, the project was soon dropped, possibly because Triumph was developing a fairly similar sort of car based on Bullet: the longer-wheelbase 2 + 2 Lynx fastback coupe.

ADO21

At least, in 1970, both ADO70 and ADO68 were under serious consideration by British Leyland, and a third, potentially much more exciting project was added. This time, and right from the outset, this third attempt was considered as a new MG sports car. This was ADO21, a mid-engined coupe styled by Harris Mann at Longbridge. The full-scale clay model submitted for consideration in Novem-

. . . to the new MGB sports car which was launched in 1962.

BMC's design department at Longbridge, in co-operation with Pininfarina, finally came up with this version of ADO34. This prototype still exists.

ber 1970 was dramatic but better balanced and more elegant than Harris' subsequent TR7 design.

The proportions were typical of mid-engined cars, with the passenger compartment well forward, sloping bonnet and raked windscreen almost flowing into one, and a high rear deck flanked by flying buttresses with a shallow, in-set rear window. Project ADO21 featured pop-up headlamps and cast-alloy wheels. In mechanical terms, a proposal to use a de Dion rear axle was of interest. The car was packaged around the overhead camshaft E-series engines, probably either the four-cylinder 1,750cc or the six-cylinder 2,200cc versions. These engines might have been the most disappointing aspect of a potentially quite exciting specification.

As a project, ADO21 had little to do with Abingdon and more with corporate British Leyland thinking. It is not even certain that the car would have been built in the MG factory if it had seen production, although it most likely would have carried the MG badge

which was used on the nose and wheels of the styling model.

There was growing uncertainty within engineering circles of British Leyland whether the mid-engined route was the correct one to take. One of the corporation's safety engineers expressed the view that in case of an accident, the driver of a mid-engined car would assume the unenviable position of the beef in a hamburger. Studies carried out by British Leyland in the American market also seemed to indicate a preference for conventional front-engined sports cars – although many American customers seemed to like the idea of a conventional car which looked like a mid-engined car.

TRIUMPH WINS AGAIN

The result was that this final MG proposal was dropped, and Triumph's Bullet project won the day. As is well known, however, the styling which was finally accepted for the TR7 – the dramatic wedge shape which brought the requested mid-engined look to the car – came from Harris Mann. After the TR7 had reached its final form, the two MG models clearly lived on borrowed time. Even so, some consideration was given to marketing badge-engineered MG versions of both the TR7 and the Lynx. Both proposals were, indeed, photographed for the record in the styling studio; the MG-badged TR7 even carried the old MG name of Magna.

None of the later projects, however, would have been Spridget replacements. After ADO70 was dropped, there does not seem to have been any serious plans for a new small sports car. ADO21 and the Bullet/TR7 derivatives were always more realistic if viewed as MGB replacements. While British Leyland still held a leading position in the small sports car. ADO21 and the Bullet/TR7 derivatives were always more realistic if viewed company lost the initiative in this market sector, which then passed first to the Italian Fiat company, and ultimately to the new Japanese contenders.

9 Spridgets in the Marketplace

When the Austin-Healey Sprite was first conceived thirty-five years ago, no one in the motor industry thought seriously in terms of market research. Len Lord probably had a notion that a small, cheap sports car would be a useful addition to the BMC range, and Donald Healey (with his vast experience of the American sports car market) probably realized that the demise of the T-series MG had left a vacuum which could be profitably exploited. There was no question, however, of sending out earnest young researchers with clip boards to interview Mr and Mrs Average, nor was the Sprite ever subjected to styling clinics, nor indeed were any of the other tools of modern market research ever employed. It is perhaps just as well, otherwise we might never have seen the Sprite and Midget in production! Instead, Donald and Geoffrey Healey simply got on with the job, designing the Sprite according to the only two constraints imposed on the project:

1. To use standard BMC components.
2. To make the bodyshell simple and cheap to produce.

As we know from history, the Sprite and Midget were successful, so the conclusion is that at the time, Len Lord and Donald Healey had been correct in their seat-of-the-pants assessment of what the market wanted. Of course, the Spridget was never a mainstream product for BMC; instead it was what we would now call an example of niche marketing. But the nice thing about BMC in its heyday was that the company was never afraid to explore such possibilities, and as a result made some very interesting cars. Sometimes they were extremely successful with this approach – what was the Mini originally, if not a classic example of niche marketing?

Once BMC had hit upon a successful formula, they were extremely reluctant to change it. Very many BMC models were kept in production for far too long. In the best of worlds, the Spridget could have been expected to have a useful production life of around ten years. It should therefore have been replaced at the latest in 1971. However, the fate of BMC from 1966 onwards, and the merger with Leyland in 1968, prevented any serious thought being given to a new Spridget – although a veritable gaggle of sports car projects was considered from time to time (*see* Chapter 8). From 1971 onwards, British Leyland was content to continue manufacturing the Midget for as long as it would sell in reasonable numbers, with the minimum amount of development work.

In the early years, BMC enjoyed what amounted to a virtual monopoly of the small sports car market. It is indicative that some of the highest annual production figures were reached by the Sprite on its own in 1959 and 1960. Then came the very serious set-back in the American market in 1960–1961, and in 1962 Triumph brought out the Spitfire which

(Right)   Designed completely without the benefit of market research, the Frog-eye Sprite soon established its own niche in the sports car market world-wide.

Where they all went. Austin-Healeys and Spridgets awaiting shipment at Cardiff docks in 1961; destination, North America.

promptly took a very large slice of the Spridget market sector, both at home and abroad.

The Spridget and the Spitfire became eternal rivals, and it is quite instructive to compare their annual production figures, as well as their UK retail prices year after year. The Spitfire was almost always a little bit more expensive than the Spridget, but tempted customers with its roomier cockpit, more comfortable appointments, and greater style. There was very little to choose between the two cars in terms of performance. While the Spitfire was originally inferior in roadholding and handling, the position became re-

versed in the 1970s, when Triumph's engineers tamed the Spitfire's swing axles, while the Midget suffered from the increased ride height of the Midget 1500. The Spitfire customer could also specify an overdrive, a luxury which was always denied the Midget purchaser.

THE US MARKET

The biggest single market for both the Spridget and the Spitfire was the USA, with considerable numbers also being sold in Canada. This of course is true of almost all

An early Triumph Spitfire Mark I – the biggest rival of the Spridget.

British post-war sports cars. With the numbers sold in North America, it is quite simply impossible to maintain the fiction that all American buyers of sports cars were enthusiasts. (Many of them per force became enthusiasts but that is a different story!) Small British sports cars sold well in America because they were different and had a novelty value. They often sold not on the strength of being sports cars, but because they were imports. Small imported cars were fashionable, regardless of whether they were MGs or VWs. Import cars sold as second (or third, even fourth) cars. They sold to women buyers. And because they were cheaper to buy and run than domestic cars, they sold to young single people.

In the USA, the small British sports cars such as the Spridgets were bought by far more college kids than could ever have afforded them in the UK. The youthful image of the Spridget as far as the American market was concerned was eventually cleverly exploited in US market sales literature for late-model Midgets. There you find gems such as the windsurfing brochure, the skateboarding brochure and the back-packing brochure, all showing the Midget against a backdrop of bright young things involved in these physical but wholesome activities.

The Power of Advertising

The absolute nadir in terms of selling techniques was reached with the sales brochure for the round-arch Midget of 1972 to 1974 which showed the car – bronze yellow, of course – surrounded by stock cars and drag racers. The models were attired in delightful period costumes as well: he had long hair, a flowery shirt and bell-bottom trousers, while she had even longer hair, a tie-dyed T-shirt (no bra, of course) and hot pants held in place by a four-inch wide belt. The slogan on the cover was 'The Great British Sports Car' and they managed to pack quite a few innuendoes into the scanty text.

Most of the advertising was predictable and pedestrian as well, although for a brief period in the 1970s, someone managed to come up with one or two quite catchy slogans for MGs. A famous one was 'You can do it in an MG' (I believe there was actually quite a famous divorce case which centred on exactly whether you *could* do it in an MG, or whether the steering-wheel was too much in the way). The Midget advertisement showed a dubious-looking male charming his way out of 'Lovely Rita Meter Maid' giving him a parking fine.

Then there was the 'Your Mother Wouldn't Like It' series of advertisements. The memorable one depicted an MG Midget parked at the kerb by the notorious coffee stall on Chelsea Bridge, debbie-type girl and companion taking much-needed refreshment after a long night out on town. It was not specified whether Mummy objected to MG Midget or to boyfriend – probably the latter: he looked like a right lounge lizard.

Bearing in mind that a sizeable proportion of Spridget buyers were always women, it would have been just retribution if sales of the model had dwindled to nothing after the sexist approach to marketing described above. It was typical that the advertising view of female liberation in the early 1970s had not got further than bra-burning. Come to think of it, I do not suppose we have really progressed a lot further since then.

I suspect that the high proportion of women Sprite owners at one time did penetrate BMC's corporate consciousness, and typically they responded by making the 1961 Sprite Mark II available in pink.

In contrast to the aggressive advertising style of the 1970s, one turns with relief to the original 1958 Frog-eye Sprite brochure, with its wonderful colour drawings so typical of the period.

The final Spitfire was this 1500 model, made until 1980.

There was even a film about the love affair between American college kids and MG sports cars – appropriately called 'Love Story' (or have I got that slightly wrong?).

THE UK MARKET

In the UK, simple economics militated against most young people buying Spridgets or other sports cars. Even if parental indulgence was forthcoming, the insurance companies were likely to throw a spanner in the works by refusing cover, or quoting exorbitant premiums, to young drivers. Being sports cars, Spridgets were not popular with insurance companies, who sometimes seemed unable to judge the performance of various types of car with accuracy and fairness. Only in old age and very second-hand

condition did Spridgets eventually get into the hands of young people in any number.

It is probable that there was a higher proportion of sports car enthusiasts who bought Spridgets in the home market than in most export markets. The ploy was normally to link the Spridget with the model's sporting achievements, whether real or imagined, in the home market sales brochures. For instance, the first MG brochure in 1961 devoted a double-page spread to the sporting heritage of the MG Midget, and race track or paddock scenes were common backdrops.

THE AUSTRALIAN MARKET

There were few markets outside the UK and North America which took the Spridgets in any quantity. Because of restrictions, the Australian market grew increasingly difficult to penetrate for British cars, unless they were assembled locally with a stipulated percentage of local content. Therefore, the Spridgets were sent down under in CKD form, starting with the Frog-eye in 1959. The Australian market continued to take Sprites until 1966, with only the occasional fully-assembled Midget being brought in from Britain. In that year, however, BMC Australia decided to switch from Sprite to Midget, to tie in more with their marketing of MGBs, also locally assembled.

Australian-assembled Midgets continued in production until 1971 when it became impossible to meet the Australian government's ever-increasing requirement for local content to avoid paying import duty. Although the numbers involved were overall quite small, the Spridget was described as the best-selling sports car in Australia in *Wheels* magazine for December 1970. Actual figures for production of CKD cars will be found in Appendix 2, pages 219–222, and it may be assumed that all right-hand drive CKD kits after 1966 were for Australia.

THE EUROPEAN MARKET

In Europe, BMC always had their best markets in the smaller, non-car producing countries: Scandinavia, the Benelux countries, Switzerland, Austria and Portugal as well as Eire. However, none of these took very many sports cars, and the best European market for Austin-Healeys and MGs was always Germany, mainly because of the numbers sold to UK and US servicemen!

Virtually all European countries had separate dealer networks for Austin and Nuffield products before the BMC-Leyland merger in 1968, and there were even fewer shared outlets than in the home market. The German importers were Woodhouse of Cologne for Nuffield products. Woodhouse were, in fact, enthusiastic MG dealers even in the 1930s which was a, shall we say, difficult time for any car importer in Germany. They are still in existence, as retail dealers for Toyota... Austin products were handled by Brüggemann in Düsseldorf. Both were eventually replaced by a wholly-owned British Leyland subsidiary, now trading as Rover Deutschland at Neuss.

There was also a good market for sports cars in France, but the situation there was complicated by the fact that Austin had several different importers, each jealously guarding his own territory. The Spridgets were not sold in Italy, to leave the field clear for the Innocenti Spider referred to in Chapter 3. Of the European markets, several had local assembly operations of BMC-supplied CKD kits, but apparently the only European country to assemble Spridgets was Eire, and the numbers were always insignificant.

THE COMMON MARKET

Then there was something called the Common Market. The British motor industry collectively was a fervent supporter of an early British entry, and de Gaulle's famous rebuff to Alec Douglas-Home in 1963 was a great disappointment to British motor manufacturers. It was also undoubtedly a major contributory factor to the gradual decline of the British motor industry afterwards. Denied membership of the EEC until Ted Heath dragged a reluctant nation into the Common Market in 1973, Britain had to make do with membership of the European Free Trade Association (EFTA), which otherwise consisted of the Scandinavian countries, Switzerland, Austria and Portugal. The advantage of lower tariffs given to British cars in these countries was helpful when it came to selling bread-and-butter cars, but none of these markets were promising as sports car outlets.

*Despite increasingly critical magazine reports, the rubber bumper Midget
continued to sell well both in the UK and in the USA.*

The round-arch Midget was another best-selling model, and one which has acquired its own following in the classic car world.

Another major change in 1964 was the all-new dashboard, with the two small dials in the centre, and the larger dials angled slightly towards each other. This steering-wheel is not the original. The new door trims and seats may also be seen. The seats, let it be said, should be the same colour as the rest of the interior trim!

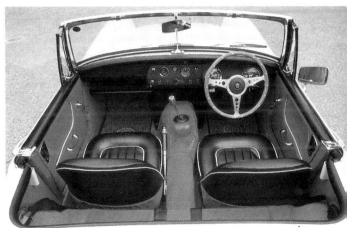

It may be mentioned that Triumph stole a march on BMC, in that going back to the 1950s, Standard-Triumph had a successful assembly operation in Belgium, supplying large quantities of cars – including sports cars such as the Spitfire – to a variety of EEC countries, at preferential rates of duty. BMC of course had the Innocenti connection in Italy, but Innocenti never made much of an impression in other European countries. By the time Britain entered the Common Market in 1973, Spridgets were distinctly old-hat and were not sold in any export market other than North America.

THE COMPETITORS

Because of the twin distribution networks operated by BMC, the Sprite and Midget often competed against each other! As is apparent from the production figure tables, Sprite output fell drastically when the Midget was introduced, then for a period the two models were almost equally popular, with the Midget only gaining the ascendancy when the Sprite was withdrawn from export markets in 1969. The detailed tables of Sprite and Midget prices show that BMC for a long time adhered to the idea of the Midget as the 'de-luxe' model of the Sprite, worth another £10 of the customer's money on the basic price. Only in 1969 did BMC price the two cars identically. The experiment of marketing a very basic standard model of the Sprite in 1961–1962 was not repeated; very few customers took the opportunity of saving £10 on basic price by foregoing bumpers, rev counter and other items of equipment.

The table comparing Spridget and Spitfire production (*see* page 215) shows that the Spitfire was the more popular car. From 1962 to 1980, Triumph made just over 314,000 Spitfires compared to some 305,000 Spridgets built over the comparable period from 1961 to 1979. (As far as we know, both the Spridget and Spitfire production figures include all

CKD kits assembled abroad, but the production of the Innocenti Spyder has been excluded from the Spridget total.) Between them, BMC and Triumph had the small sports car market sewn up. After the merger, British Leyland enjoyed a virtual monopoly of this market sector, as indeed they did of the entire sports car market.

The Specialist Car Makers

All of the remaining small British sports cars were the products of tiny specialist manufacturers, who relied on buying in major mechanical components from BMC, Triumph or Ford. These small manufacturers had minimal production capacity and few if any dealer outlets, and could only compete with the Spridget/Spitfire on price by selling their cars in kit form, thereby avoiding Purchase Tax. For instance, a Lotus Super Seven cost £645 in kit form in 1962, virtually the same as a complete Spridget, and no less than £868 in complete built-up form. The Mini-Marcos of 1966 cost £645 in kit form – at that time more than a complete Spridget. The Morgan 4/4 was the traditional answer to a Spridget but was always more expensive, and was gradually moved up-market. By 1964, the 4/4 had acquired a 1,500cc Ford engine and cost £755, more than £100 more than the Spridget.

The tendency was always for the specialist car makers to move their products upmarket, not surprisingly as it is important for these small concerns to maximize the profit per unit.

Others took the route of providing a slightly different type of car. Bond bravely brought out a small four-seater GT, the Triumph Herald-based Equipe, in 1963, but at £786 it was quite expensive and well outside the Spridget bracket. There were other cars in a similar vein, but their *raison d'être* was largely taken away in January 1969 when Ford introduced the Capri, a 1,300cc basic version of which sold for £890.

It may not have been a sports car, but for an extra £120 over the Midget it offered four-seater accommodation, a roof and a very comparable performance.

The GTi Generation

What really undermined the small sports car market, particularly in the 1970s, was the emergence of sporting derivatives of small saloons. These would often out-perform the ragtops, could be as much fun to drive, and for a similar outlay offered a great deal more convenience for everyday use. BMC of course had been early in the field with the Mini-Cooper, while Ford's Lotus-Cortina and Vauxhall's Brabham Viva followed the same pattern. Soon, there were GT badges everywhere. Towards the end of the 1970s, with the growing popularity of fuel injection systems, GTi became the fashionable letters (spearheaded by the VW Golf GTi) and Turbo became another coveted badge. The Midget and the Spitfire continued unchanged, being totally overtaken by such modern developments.

Japanese Competition

It must also be admitted that Britain, to some degree, lost the initiative in the sports car market to foreign concerns. In an eerie preview of the situation which prevails in the 1990s, three Japanese manufacturers all brought out sports cars in the early 1960s, although none were as accomplished as their present-day offerings.

Datsun (Nissan) brought out their first sports model as early as 1959, under the name of Fairlady, but only when a second-generation Fairlady appeared in 1962 did it make any impact. This was a 1.6-litre model whose styling made it look like an MGB or Spridget clone. Usually known in export markets as the 1600 Sports, this car sold in some numbers in the USA, where it was soon discovered that its engine had some parts interchangeability with the BMC B-series unit. (Datsun had based their original design on the engine from the Austin Somerset and Cambridge models which they had assembled in the mid-1950s.)

Eventually, the Fairlady name was transferred to the first of the Z-series coupes in 1969, which quickly moved into the sector of the market recently vacated by the Austin-Healey 3000 in the USA. Toyota's early offering was the 800 Sports with an air-cooled flat-twin engine and styling which foreshadowed the later and more famous 2000GT. Neither the Datsun nor the Toyota made any impression in Europe.

However, Honda's first car, introduced in 1962, did make it to Europe and to the UK. This small, open two-seater was technologically very advanced with many features based on Honda's extremely successful motorcyles. With twin overhead camshafts and four carburettors, the tiny 531cc engine developed an amazing 44bhp. In the early years, the S500 had independent rear-wheel suspension with individual chain-drive to each rear wheel – the chain-enclosing cases acting as longitudinal trailing arms – while later versions had a conventional rear-end set-up. The engine grew to 791cc and 70bhp, and a coupe version was brought out. These were tiny cars. They were less than 10ft (3m) in length and correspondingly narrow, and were built to fit in with the unique Japanese legislation which bases vehicle taxation on exterior dimensions. In consequence, the interior was somewhat cramped, especially for average-sized westerners. Production was always on a small scale, and comparatively few cars were sold in the UK, where the S800 nevertheless attracted, and retains, a devoted following.

Continental Competition

More important in the 1960s and 1970s, however, were the efforts of European manufacturers. In the pre-Capri days, undisputed

Italian challenge of the 1970s: the business end of a Fiat X1/9 . . .

leader of the 'sporty' coupe brigade was the VW Karmann Ghia, which I once described as neither a classic nor a sports car, but which was enormously successful in its own right. Moreover, I am certain that it was quite often considered as a Spridget alternative in the American market, where in 1973 it cost $2,800 compared to the $2,699 asked for the Midget, and the $2,895 for the Spitfire.

Many other Continental manufacturers offered cars in a similar mould, notably the Renault Floride/Caravelle series. But the Karmann Ghia and its imitators were considered distinctly non-U in the sports car world. On the other hand, no one could deny the impeccable heritage of Fiat in the small sports car field, going back to the Ballila Sports of the mid-1930s. In its day, the Ballila was an effective competitor in club-level racing for the then-current MG Midgets.

Fiat usually had one or two open sports two-seaters in their vast catalogue, but some of them were more inspired than others. The 1955 1100TV sports cabriolet was pretty awful but by 1960 had developed into the much-better 1500 with a twin overhead cam engine. This was just pretty, and the same

could be said of the little 850 Spyder of 1965–1973, styled by Bertone, which endeared itself to many owners (notwithstanding its humble origin and rear engine). It was something of a rarity in the UK, and it was not offered with right-hand drive. The year 1966 saw the 124 Sport Special in coupe and spyder forms, fitted with 1.4- and later 1.6-litre twin-cam engines, of which the spyder, later built and marketed by Pininfarina, was to have a long and distinguished career.

THE ITALIAN REVOLUTION

In 1972, however, Fiat brought out an even more interesting car, the X1/9. This used the powerpack from Fiat's transverse-engined front-wheel drive 128 saloon, mounted behind the seats. The body was styled by Bertone. The result was an attractive and neat two-seater with integral roll bar and removable targa-type roof panel. With a 1,290cc engine developing 75bhp, the original X1/9 was good for 100mph (160kph) and scored high marks for its roadholding and handling.

. . . and the baton passes to Japan, with the 1984 Toyota MR2.

It was very much the sort of car that many enthusiasts had hoped British Leyland would bring out. Ironically, it was also in many respects similar to the Healey WAEC project of the mid-1960s (*see* Chapter 8). Although not the first mid-engined sports car, the X1/9 was a much better all-rounder than the Lotus Europa or the controversial VW-Porsche 914, scoring high marks for practicality in everyday use. It was described as the most significant sports car since the Datsun 240Z.

Sophistication usually has its price, and when official right-hand drive X1/9s finally appeared in Britain in February 1977, the retail price was £2,997, almost £1,000 more than the Midget, and more than the MGB. In the USA, the X1/9 was also more expensive than the MGB, but cost appreciably less than the TR7 ($4,947 against the $5,649 asked for the Triumph in 1976). Later X1/9s were fitted with 1,500cc engines and also had five-speed gearboxes. Like the 124 Spyder before it, the X1/9 was eventually farmed out, in this case to Bertone, and just went on and on. It was estimated that by 1987, more than 200,000 had been made.

Eventually, the X1/9 was out-gunned by Toyota's MR2 of 1984, still with us but now in its second set of clothes. Interest in sports cars generally was revived in the late 1980s, with the Mazda MX-5 (Miata) and the new Lotus Elan, while the Reliant Scimitar SST failed to make much of an impression. Sadly, however, all of these are really rather expensive cars. By extrapolation of the price development of the Sprite and Midget from 1958 until 1981, a 1991 version should cost around £8,000, yet the average price of the cars mentioned is almost twice as much as that.

Is it that the day of the budget sports car is definitely over? Or is it that no manufacturer is brave enough to make such a car in sufficiently large numbers to keep the price down? The truth is probably that while it would be possible to make a true low-cost sports car, such a car would now seem so primitive that it would only have a very limited following. If motoring essentials of the 1990s include anti-lock brakes, power steering, four-wheel drive – not to mention central locking, electric windows, stereo, alloy wheels and a car alarm – it is hard to see a return to the concept of the original Frogeye Sprite, with its loose sidescreens, packaway hood and the heater only an option.

10   The Spridget in Motor Sports

Barely had the Frog-eye been introduced before the new model made its first appearance in a competitive event. Three Sprites were entered in the Alpine Rally in July 1958, and immediately established the new model in the sporting world by finishing first, second and third in class. The class winner was John Sprinzel who also finished fifteenth overall, although at the end of the rally the Sprite had neither an exhaust system nor shock absorbers. Additionally, Sprinzel and co-driver Willy Cave had cut a hole in the bonnet to be able to put in oil and water, as the bonnet had jammed after a collision with a milestone. On top of everything else, the car at one stage caught fire, yet came through to win its class, which speaks volumes for the stamina of both car and crew.

John Sprinzel (born 1930)

The most miraculous thing is that John Sprinzel could fit into a Sprite at all, being around 6ft 5in (1.95m) tall. (Perhaps this was what prompted him to develop a coupe version with more head-room!)

Very much a man of the world with a cosmopolitan outlook, Sprinzel has German, French and Portuguese ancestors, and was born in Germany near the Polish border. This accounts for his gifts as a linguist. His family came to England while he was still of tender years. He was a pilot in the RAF and studied economics before joining his father's business of silk screen printing and transfer manufacturing.

His first rally was the 1955 RAC, for which he borrowed his mother's Austin A30, apparently without telling her what he was going to use it for. Since his father and sister crewed for him, the secret was soon revealed. He then bought his own rally car, a Triumph TR2, and was asked to join the BMC team, driving an Austin A35. When the Sprite appeared in 1958, Sprinzel took to it like a duck to water, and for the next few years Sprinzel and Sprite were almost synonymous.

He founded the Speedwell tuning firm which specialized in A35s and later Sprites. When leaving Speedwell he became for a time associated with Donald Healey at Warwick, but eventually set up his own firm of John Sprinzel Racing. He developed and marketed the much-modified Frog-eye based Sebring Sprite coupe, which became a legend in its own right.

After the Sprite days, Sprinzel rallied a variety of other makes, and had drives with works teams, including Triumph, Ford, SAAB and Datsun. He wrote a book on *Modified Motoring* and followed this up with a not altogether serious look at international rallying, *Sleepless Knights*. He became rallying correspondent to the *Daily Mirror* and contributed to BLMC's *High Road* magazine. He also became a television commentator on motor sport.

Sprinzel's last association with the Spridget came when he took a Midget on the London–Sydney marathon in 1968. When the next great marathon came round, the 1970 World Cup Rally, Sprinzel was in the organizer's seat rather than a competitor.

Sprinzel started out as a gentleman amateur but became a devoted professional, while always retaining a sense of proportion and never taking anything too seriously. A bon vivant with a taste for the good things in life, Sprinzel's charm and enthusiasm endeared him to contemporaries, but he also acquired a reputation for lack of prudence and a taste for boyish pranks!

SPRINZEL'S PMO 200

The Sprinzel car for the 1958 Alpine was registered under PMO 200, which became one of the most famous number-plates to grace a Sprite. John Sprinzel became the best known and most successful of the Sprite drivers, in rallying as well as track racing. Among the subsequent rally results scored by Sprinzel was a fourteenth place overall in the 1959 Monte Carlo Rally and class wins in the 1959 and 1960 Liège-Rome-Liège Rallies, coupled with a third place overall on the latter occasion.

On home ground, Sprinzel and co-driver Richard Bensted-Smith came second overall in the 1960 RAC Rally, coupled with a class win. One of Sprinzel's final appearances in a Sprite was in the 1962 Monte Carlo Rally, together with Christabel Carlisle, finishing fourth in class. The car was still PMO 200, but it was now a fully-developed Sebring Sprite (*see* Chapter 3).

There was one more memorable outing for John Sprinzel. In the London–Sydney marathon in December 1968, Sprinzel and Roy Fidler entered an 'old' MG Midget – probably a 1966 model – which proudly carried Sprinzel's cherished number-plate, PMO 200. The appearance of the car was somewhat distorted by a foot-high fuel tank on the roof of the hard-top. PMO 200 was fitted with a five-speed racing gearbox, fibreglass body panels, and Minilite wheels. With very little in the way of sponsorship, they hoped to win the special award for private entrants, and did remarkably well throughout the European and Asian stages, only to be forced into retirement when the front suspension on one side collapsed on the final Australian stage. Repairs put the Sprinzel car well outside the permitted time limit, although the Midget was able to make its way to Sydney under its own power.

Sprinzel was the most consistent Sprite driver in the early days, but mention must

John Sprinzel and Christabel Carlisle on their way to Monte Carlo with PMO 200 in 1962.

Always popular with amateurs in club level events, this Frog-eye is part of a mixed batch of cars about to start in the London Motor Club's Little Rally in 1959.

also be made of Gold and Hughes who took a Frog-eye to a second place overall in the 1959 RAC Rally; Moore who was second in the 1959 Scottish Rally; and Boyd and Johnston who were the winners of the 1960 Circuit of Ireland – the only victory for a Frog-eye in a major rally. BMC's Competitions Department never made any great use of the Sprite or later the Midget. Sprinzel was occasionally listed as an official BMC entrant, while Pat Moss and Ann Wisdom had a couple of entries in a Sprite, no doubt finding light relief from their usual Austin-Healey 3000 mount! They were much less successful in the smaller car, however, their best result being a second in class in the 1960 RAC Rally.

BMC did run three Midgets in the 1961 RAC Rally and were awarded first and second in class – Derek Astle and Roberts also finishing eighth overall. There were a few more rally appearances for works Midgets in 1962, but after that BMC concentrated on the Big Healeys and the phenome-

A bit of hill-climbing did not come amiss either, as here at Wiscombe Park in 1961. The Frog-eye looks very much the part, apart from a somewhat incongruous radio aerial!

Standard Frog-eye dicing with Sebring Sprite coupe at Silverstone in 1961.

*The later models were less frequently seen in action, but here is an early
Midget at Silverstone in 1961.*

Alternatively you might do a bit of mud-plugging with your Sprite Mark III.

nal Mini-Coopers. The later Spridgets did not appear so frequently as private entries in rallies either, although Woodside and Crawford won the Circuit of Ireland in a Sprite Mark II in 1963.

SPRITES AT SEBRING

The 12-hour race held at Sebring from 1952 onwards had become the premier American sports car race; in its own way as important as the Le Mans 24-hour race. The venue was the old airfield at Sebring in Florida and the event took place in March of each year. Donald and Geoffrey Healey had plenty of experience with this race, where Austin-Healeys had competed regularly since 1954. For the 1959 race, they decided to enter three Sprites, secure in the knowledge that a good performance here would be a vital boost to the new model's sales in the USA, although they may not have realized that they were also starting a legend!

The original 1959 Sebring cars were somewhat modified from standard. They featured specially tuned engines, wire wheels and Dunlop disc brakes, and were fitted with the Jensen-made Healey-style hard-tops. Four of these cars were built, of which three ran in the race. The organization of the team entry was undertaken by BMC's American importers, Hambro, and an all-American team of drivers was selected, of whom John Colgate was to have a long association with the racing Sprites. The three Sprites finished first, second and third in class, the highest-placed car coming thirty-first overall. After the race, the cars were sold to various BMC and Austin-Healey distributors in the States.

In 1960, the Sebring organizers instituted a four-hour race for small GT cars which had to be to standard homologated specification. For this race, Healey entered the Sprite which had contested the 1959 Targa Florio, and got none other than Stirling Moss to drive it. Moss finished a very close second after a rather quicker Italian Abarth twin-cam car.

In the 1960 12-hour race, a more special Sprite was entered for John Sprinzel to drive. This car had a fibreglass body and Dunlop disc brakes on all four wheels. After a blown cylinder head gasket was replaced early in the race, Sprinzel and co-driver Lumkin went on to win their class.

The line-up of BMC sports cars for the 1968 Sebring race, including the class-winning fuel-injected Sprite coupe and the 'Midget' which came fifteenth overall, as well as an MGB GT and one of the lightweight MGC CTs.

More Sebring Action

There was an impressive line-up of Sprites for the 1961 Sebring races. The official BMC/Healey team ran four Sprites in the four-hour race and two in the 12-hour race, while John Sprinzel fielded two of his Sebring Sprite coupes which ran in both races. The Healey-prepared Sprites had outwardly standard-looking bodies which were in fact moulded in fibreglass. They were driven by Walt Hansgen, Bruce McLaren, Ed Leavens and Briggs Cunningham, while the Sprinzel cars were driven by Stirling Moss and Pat Moss in the four-hour race.

The Sprites were again beaten by the Abarth, but all six cars finished the four-hour race, in third to eighth places, with Walt Hansgen being the highest placed driver. The Sprinzel car driven by Stirling Moss was inevitably registered as PMO 200! In the 12-hour race, the two Warwick-prepared cars were second and third in class (fifteenth and twenty-fifth overall), while John Sprinzel trailed behind at thirty-seventh overall. John Colgate co-drove with Ed Leavens on one of the Warwick cars.

Big-name drivers again featured in the Sprites in the 1962 Sebring entry list. Healeys at Warwick had produced four cars for the four-hour race. These were based on the new Mark II Sprite, but with light-alloy bodies, Healey's own hard-tops, wire wheels and 998cc engines. Just one car was prepared for the 12-hour race, with a light-alloy coupe body and a 1,098cc engine. Stirling Moss, Pedro Rodriguez, Innes Ireland and the film star Steve McQueen drove the Sprites in the four-hour race, finishing third, sixth, seventh and ninth overall – again bested by the Abarths. Steve McQueen and John Colgate were co-drivers of the single car entered in the 12-hour race, and were leading the class when half-way through the race the centre main-bearing went and the car had to retire.

In 1963, the small GT car race was shortened to three hours. The Healey team ran two of the 1962 race cars, although one had mysteriously changed its identity to an MG Midget, still wearing the 9252 WD registration from the previous year! This car was driven by Graham Hill, and the second car by Pedro Rodriguez. Both were early retirements with broken differentials.

The single Sprite running in the 12-hour race also had its own share of problems. This was the 1962 1,098cc coupe, driven by John Colgate and Clive Baker. They retired, suffering from a fractured oil pipe and the cylinder block cracking around the centre mainbearing, while leading their class and with only an hour to go before the finish. A similar fate overtook the Colgate/Baker Sprite coupe in the 1964 Sebring 12-hour race, the only Sprite to be entered at Sebring in this year.

Last Laps at Sebring

Better fortunes attended the Sprites in their final appearances at Sebring from 1965 to 1969. Both cars entered in 1965 had 1,293cc engines. One of the cars had the aerodynamic body specially developed for Le Mans; this was driven by Clive Baker and Rauno Aaltonen to fifteenth place overall and first in class. Two other members of BMC's rally team, Timo Makinen and Paddy Hopkirk, took the older-style coupe to eighteenth place, while an MG Midget driven by Andrew Hedges and Roger Mac won the GT class and was twenty-sixth overall.

Two of the Le Mans type cars were entered in 1966; Timo Makinen and Paul Hawkins finished eighteenth overall and won their class, while Rauno Aaltonen and Clive Baker were second in class. Next year, it was the turn of Aaltonen and Baker to take the class honours, finishing also thirteenth overall – the highest-ever overall placing for a Spridget in the Sebring 12-hour race – while a very standard-looking production Sprite, driven by Roger Enever, Alec Poole and Carson Baird, finished 18th overall.

The year 1968 saw the last Sebring entry for the official BMC/Healey team, as the BMC competitions department was shortly to undergo major changes as a result of the Leyland merger. One of the streamlined Sprite coupes, now with a fuel injection engine, was driven by Clive Baker and Mike Garton. Despite problems with water in the fuel, they managed to continue the tradition by taking a class win. The only other entry was an MG Midget – which in reality was a Sprite – driven by Jerry Truitt and Randy Canfield. They finished fifteenth overall and won the sports car class.

The last appearance for the Spridgets at Sebring came in 1969, when American privateer Jim Baker of Atlanta, Georgia, fielded two Sprites, scoring a first and second in class. The 1969 Sebring race was also the farewell appearance for the MGB and MGC. An MGB GT and the two lightweight MGC GT cars, run by the American BMC importers, all finished but not spectacularly well.

THE TARGA FLORIO STORY

The Sprite's career in the famous Sicilian road race was patchier. A little modified Frog-eye had been run by Tommy Wisdom and Bernard Cahier in the 1959 race. The only problem they encountered was that the throttle cable broke on the last lap, so Wisdom had to drive the car on the ignition switch. It did not prevent him from finishing seventeenth overall, although without this mishap he would likely have done better still. As previously mentioned, this was the very same car that Stirling Moss drove at Sebring in 1960.

There was then a hiatus until 1964 before a Sprite appeared in the Targa Florio again. This was a much more special car, with a light alloy body on a standard Spridget platform, and also fitted with semi-elliptic rear springs which were only just coming into

production on the Sprite Mark III. The 1964 Targa Florio car was originally built as an open two-seater with a characteristic Kamm-style tail, although this car was later fitted with a fastback hard-top. In the race, the car was driven by Tommy Wisdom and Paddy Hopkirk, but soon retired with a broken half shaft.

A similar-looking special car was built for the 1965 Targa Florio, driven by Rauno Aaltonen and Clive Baker. In addition, the BMC competitions department entered one of the special MG Midget GT coupes (of which more later) which was driven by Paddy Hopkirk and Andrew Hedges. The Midget finished eleventh overall, while the Sprite was delayed by problems with the front disc brakes and eventually finished fifteenth overall.

The 1965 Sprite open two-seater was rebuilt as a coupe for the 1966 Targa Florio, and was again driven by Aaltonen and Baker. In a curious repeat of the 1964 race, the car broke a half shaft, but since a spare was carried, Clive Baker was able to replace the broken shaft with a little help from a pair of English spectators! The car eventually finished sixteenth overall. A 1,293cc-engined coupe was built for Baker and Aaltonen to run in the 1967 Targa Florio but the car was involved in a collision with a spectator who walked across the circuit.

No luck attended the single Sprite entered in the 1968 race either. Although based on a standard production car, this had a 1,293cc dry-sump lubricated engine and a five-speed gearbox. Aaltonen and Baker were again the drivers but had to retire with a blown engine after overheating and losing water. The car later ran in the Mugello road race, winning its class in the hands of Baker and Andrew Hedges.

A final racing Sprite was built for the 1969 Targa Florio, but without support from British Leyland it was impossible for the Healeys to enter on their own. The car was fitted with a fuel injection engine and had an all-aluminium open body. It was subsequently sold to the Austin-Healey and MG distributor of West Palm Beach in Florida, Ed Bussey.

THE LE MANS SPRITES

The 24-hour race at Le Mans has been the most famous and prestigious of all sports car races for generations. It always had a particularly strong following among British manufacturers and in consequence among British motor sports enthusiasts. Jaguar, Bentley, Aston Martin and Lagonda have all won the race, and most other British sports car makes have taken part. Before the war, the race was contested by MG Midgets on several occasions, and at one time by a team of Austin Sevens. They were to find a modern successor in the shape of the Sprites which raced at Le Mans from 1960 to 1968.

Two special Sprites were entered for the 1960 race, but only one car was accepted, the other being on the reserve list. The 1960 Le Mans Sprites had lightweight Falcon fibre-glass bodies and 996cc engines specially developed by the Morris Engines Branch at Coventry. It was the intention to race the cars with Perspex windscreens, but the Le Mans organizers dictated the use of full-width laminated glass screens of a specified minimum height. The drivers were John Colgate and John Dalton. The car ran in the 1,000cc sports car prototype class, and despite leaking oil on to the clutch towards the end of the race it won its class, coming twentieth overall.

The 1960 Le Mans car was substantially modified for the 1961 race. It was fitted with a coupe body based on the design of the 'Super Sprite' prototype (*see* Chapter 8). This was the first of the special Sprite coupes built for racing. Another car was prepared for the Ecurie Ecosse racing team: the car which Walt Hansgen had driven in the 1961 Sebring race. The coupe was driven by John Colgate and Paul Hawkins, the Ecurie

Ecosse car by none other than one-time Le Mans winner Ninian Sanderson together with J McKay. Unfortunately, the Ecurie Ecosse car crashed, and the coupe holed a piston by mid-evening.

The Special Le Mans Coupes

There were no Sprites in the 1962 Le Mans race but another special coupe was built for 1963. It was entered for John Whitmore and Bob Olthoff, both BMC works drivers who had raced an Austin-Healey 3000 in the 1962 Le Mans. The 1963 Sprite was very quick, able to lap at 100mph (160kph), and should have done well, but during the night Bob Olthoff crashed at White House corner. There was better luck in store for the 1964 race, when a single Sprite coupe, based on the Targa Florio design, was driven by Clive Baker and Bill Bradley into twenty-fourth place overall.

Some serious thought was now devoted to making the Sprite go faster and become more competitive. Geoffrey Healey enlisted the help of Dr Weaving of the Austin Motor Company's research department, and it was arranged to have the Le Mans and Targa Florio cars tested in the wind tunnel at Longbridge. These tests indicated that there was plenty of scope for modifications, as a result of which the final and definitive Sprite racing coupe shape emerged. Although the aerodynamic shape was developed with an eye to obtaining maximum speed on the Mulsanne straight at Le Mans, the new car actually made its debut in the 1965 Sebring race as previously recounted.

Two of the new coupes were entered for the 1965 Le Mans, the drivers being Paul Hawkins/John Rhodes and Rauno Aaltonen/ Clive Baker. As originally entered, the cars were painted a fluorescent lime green, but Geoffrey Healey was told by the race organizers that this was 'dangerous' and he was obliged to have the cars re-sprayed in a more traditional dark green before the race. The

Pitstop for the Baker/Hedges Sprite at Le Mans in 1967.

Aaltonen/Baker car blew its engine on Sunday morning, but Hawkins and Rhodes finished twelfth overall and won their class. This was the best-ever Sprite result at Le Mans.

It may be added that one of the 1965 cars was restored and re-painted in the original fluorescent green colour in 1990 and duly appeared for the pre-race parade of past competitors at Le Mans, without any protests from the organizers! The wind-tunnel developed coupes had proved their worth, being timed at 147mph (236kph) on the Mulsanne straight.

Two cars were entered again in 1966, driven by Paddy Hopkirk/Andrew Hedges and Clive Baker/John Rhodes. They were very similar to the 1965 cars but were fitted with overdrive gearboxes which gave a small improvement on top speed, the cars being timed at almost 150mph (240kph). Sadly, however, both cars retired with broken connecting rods.

The year 1967 was a happier one, as the single Sprite (driven by Clive Baker and Andrew Hedges) finished fifteenth overall, and was awarded the *Motor* trophy for the highest-placed British car. The car was fitted

Spridgets are still raced in a variety of events and indeed have their own championship series organized by the MG Car Club. This race-prepared Sprite (or Midget?!) shows an interesting mix of features, but originality is less important in racing, as long as you stay within the homologation rules!

Sprite grille (1961–1969 type) but MG badge on boot-lid. 'S' registration but chrome bumpers; one-piece front bumper (pre-1970 style) but quarter rear bumpers (1970–1974). Square rear wheelarches but Rostyle wheels of the type found on the round arch car. A difficult car to identify correctly!

However mixed the parentage of this car may be, it is immaculately prepared and you can't miss this one in its striking colour scheme.

This car is fitted with the final style of Spridget hard-top, introduced for the 1969 model year and of a design very similar to the MGB hard-top.

A novel way of improving access to the engine compartment, this lift-off bonnet with external clips does tend to make life easier during those frantic pitstops.

Not quite so well-presented as the smart exterior, the under-bonnet view of the racing Spridget proves that it is very much a working car.

sports the original MG badges and green paintwork, as opposed to the Austin-Healey Sprite badges and the blue/silver colour scheme used for its disguise!

The Speedwell Coupe

The alternative record car which was truly a Sprite, was the streamlined Speedwell coupe which in 1960 set a national Belgian class G record at 212.719kph (132.206mph) over the flying kilometre. The driver was Graham Hill, and this was a remarkable result from an unsupercharged car, bearing witness to the efficiency of the Costin-designed bodywork. On the same occasion, Reg Venner-Pack of Speedwell took a Speedwell Sprite GT racer to 110.9mph (178.4kph).

Many more Sprites and Midgets appeared in national and international events than it is possible to list here. They were raced by amateur as well as professional drivers, not always with successful results but usually giving plenty of enjoyment to both drivers and spectators! In the USA, the Frog-eye Sprites were pre-eminent in the Sports Car Class of America's category H for production cars, and later Spridgets continued their successes. In 1963 Donna Mae Mims, who wore a pink racing suit to match her pink Sprite, became the national champion. In 1966 and again in 1970, MG Midgets won their class championship in SCCA racing, driven by Carson Baird and W Koch. Indeed, Sprites and Midgets are still regularly campaigned in club level racing, and have their own championship series in Britain, organized by the MG Car Club.

11 The Spridget Today

There are, literally, thousands of Spridgets still around. You may not see them everywhere, but they are still frequently encountered. Many Spridgets still work for a living, rather than being pampered and cossetted and wheeled out for the occasional *concours* event. Inevitably, the 1974–1979 Midget 1500 is the most common model still seen on the road, but the 1969–1974 period cars are far from uncommon, and the pre-1969 cars cannot be called rare either. It is only the original Frog-eye which has largely disappeared from everyday traffic. This has more to do with its greater perceived desirability and thus higher value than with actual rarity. There are plenty of Frog-eyes around; it is just that they do not come out to play as often as they used to.

The classic car boom has been with us for the best part of twenty years. Already in the early 1970s, while you could still buy a new Midget of the traditional chrome-bumper type, the Frog-eye Sprite was being thought of as a true classic car. By contrast, it has taken longer for subsequent Spridget models to gain entrance to that particular Valhalla, and it would seem that the rubber-bumper Midget 1500 is still considered somewhat of a poor relation in the company of earlier models.

A useful rule of thumb in the classic car world is that sooner or later, any MG will find its niche and become 'accepted', regardless of how controversial it was when new. So, there is still hope for the Midget 1500. Meanwhile, let us be thankful that these cars are still being preserved in substantial numbers, and are available to those who want to enjoy a traditional British sports car for a small outlay, and at modest running costs.

PRACTICALITIES

As far as using the cars today is concerned, there is perhaps less in the way of difference between the various models than might at first be thought. If you have experience of any one of the Spridget models, you will feel immediately at home in any other. A Midget 1500 may be some 15mph (20km) faster than a Frog-eye on top speed, and have better acceleration, but neither car is now likely to be driven flat-out in the traffic-light Grand Prix, and the pace at which we now do our motoring seems to be more governed by speed limits and traffic conditions than by the theoretical performance of our cars.

All of the Spridgets are entertaining cars to drive. They are simple and uncomplicated little cars, and can be run and maintained almost on a shoestring. If you approach a Spridget in the right frame of mind, owning and running one of these cars can be very enjoyable indeed – but you should not expect too much of it.

Spridgets are not flawless. For people of more than average girth or height, the biggest drawback will be the relatively cramped cockpit. Those who are 6ft tall or more will be barely comfortable and are likely to face the interesting choice of whether to look through, or over the windscreen. With the hood up, these cars can feel downright claustrophobic. In addition, they are not all that easy to get into or out of – if a modicum of dignity is to be preserved – especially not with the hood in place. However, once you have made yourself as comfortable as your stature allows, you will no doubt appreciate the intimate cosiness of the cockpit.

The low seating position, legs stretched

out in front of you, is in the best sports car tradition. You will find that the steering-wheel and facia are very close, but generally the controls are well laid out and fall easily to hand. You very quickly become familiar with the driving environment. You acquire a new perspective of the world from a Spridget: because the cars are so low, everything else seems to tower over you. Your eyes seem to be about on the same level as a bicyclist's bum, and drawing up next to a truck or a double-decker bus can be an intimidating experience and not one for the faint-hearted.

It would be wrong to say that the Spridget is the sort of car that shrinks around you. It is small, and it feels small. Like the Mini, the Spridget feels a little bit like a go-kart. With the high-geared and very direct steering, the car is agile and manoeuvrable. It is an easy car to position accurately as you nip in and out of traffic, and at the end of the journey it can be parked in spaces denied to most other cars. A Spridget is equally handy in traffic as it is around narrow country lanes. Here you can truly enjoy yourself, and the fact that the performance is in absolute terms modest does not seem to matter so much. On the other hand, it is not the sort of car that seems ideal for a 200-mile motorway journey in the rain . . .

THE CHOICE

The Frog-Eye

The purist will pick a Frog-eye. It is, after all, the true original of the range. It also commands a fairly hefty premium over any of the later models. In some respects, however, it is a surprisingly impractical car and most of the criticisms levelled against the Frog-eye thirty years ago are equally valid today.

Boot access is awkward, the hood and sidescreens are not particularly weather-proof, the one-piece bonnet and front end is cumbersome and makes it difficult to get to the engine and the battery. It is also the least powerful of all the Spridgets, and the all-round drum brakes must now count as a minus point. But the model has arguably greater charm and charisma than any later Spridget, and its once controversial looks would now be rated as cute by most observers.

If you consider a Frog-eye simply as a classic car, to be used on high days and holidays rather than in the cut-and-thrust of everyday motoring, it makes the best choice of all the Spridgets. It is also likely to have the best investment potential.

We have charted the course of steady improvement followed by the Spridgets in the 1961–1969 period (*see* Chapters 4 and 5). Strangely enough, most of these improvements, which were so much praised at the time, seem to have very little influence on most buyers today. Actually, the 1961–1962 models were very little different from the Frog-eye, except for the front- and rear-end restyling. But by comparison they look ordinary . . .

The external and lockable boot-lid must still count as a worthwhile improvement over the Frog-eye. Similarly, the disc brakes fitted from late 1962 are well worth having, even if the first 1,098cc engine, introduced at the same time, has a mixed reputation. The big-bearing version of this engine which appeared in 1964 is more robust. Whether to have the pre-1964 models with quarter-elliptic rear springs or the post-March 1964 cars with semi-elliptic springs is now not so important, but the wind-down windows of the later cars do score on practicality. One thing to bear in mind about the 1961–1966 models is that they are now actually much rarer than the Frog-eye, and the fact that they are relatively unusual should help to make them attractive to many people.

The Ultimate Spridget

The ultimate chrome-bumper Spridget is

probably the 1966–1969 Midget Mark III or Sprite Mark IV. Its much-improved hood and 1,275cc engine, combined with the un-adorned looks of the earlier cars, should make it more popular than it seems to be at the moment. Price guides to classic cars seem to rate it as the most valuable Spridget and second only to the Frog-eye. This suggests that it is sought after by the discerning, but – like the 1961–1966 period cars – it is now comparatively rare.

The 1969–1974 models with the Leyland-style face-lift are certainly much more common, at least in MG Midget form, while lovers of the obscure will delight in finding one of the rare late-model Sprites, especially one of the 1971 Austin Sprites. The round-arch Midget of the 1972–1974 period exists in plenty, and is the one of the post-Leyland models that has attracted most of a following. Remarkable how much difference a simple wheel cut-out shape can make!

The Most Affordable Spridget

The 1974–1979 rubber-bumper Midget 1500 rates lowliest in the classic car league table, and is the most affordable of all Spridgets. Its looks and its Triumph-sourced engine made it controversial when new, and this still seems to be the case. Yet, it can provide as much driving enjoyment as any other Spridget, and with the slightly more power-ful engine may be more suitable for everyday motoring. These cars can still be bought at surprisingly low costs, and they make ex-cellent starter classics for enthusiasts on a limited budget. Of all the Spridgets, it is the 1500 which provides the most fun for money, and isn't that what Spridgets are all about?

When the cars were new, the Spridget may have lost out to the Spitfire in the market place, but the Spridget had the last laugh: model for model, the Sprites and Midgets are now more sought-after and more valuable than their eternal rival. Undoubtedly this

has something to do with the ever-lasting mystique of the octagon! Where comparable models exist, there is little to choose between Sprite and Midget; only the Frog-eye is in a class of its own.

ORIGINAL: TO BE OR NOT TO BE?

This is always a vexed question in the classic car world. Disregarding for a moment the diligent research into minutiae carried out with deadly earnestness by the serious *concours* brigade, it is my personal opinion that you pick a particular classic car because, on balance, you decide that its attractions out-weigh its disadvantages, and you then accept it in its original form, warts and all. On the whole I am therefore inclined to come down on the side of keeping a car – any car – in its original form, the way that its manufacturer (however misguided!) intended. But to each man his own, and I have no quarrel with those who feel otherwise.

Modifications to Spridgets were, and to some extent still are, very common. The classic example is the wide variety of alter-native bonnets offered for the Frog-eye Sprite in its heyday. Undoubtedly, a Sprite Mark I which may still be fitted with an original contemporary Speedwell or Sprinzel bonnet makes a particularly interesting car. On the other hand, I would consider it misguided if a present-day owner were to throw away an original Frog-eye bonnet in favour of a mod-ern alternative bonnet design.

Similarly, if it is important to have disc brakes or wire wheels, I would advise you to pick a Sprite Mark III or Mark IV, rather than modifying a Frog-eye to suit your pre-ference. Many Frog-eye owners have spent much effort in trying to persuade themselves and others that their disc-braked, wire-wheeled car is an authentic Sprinzel-modified Sebring Sprite, but I fear that it is most often wishful thinking!

The calendar may say 1991 but you could easily be forgiven for thinking that it was 1961. Here is the new Healey Frogeye, the car that turns the clock back thirty years.

Here is a clue, at any rate: the Sprite badge is gone, and the badge simply says Healey Frogeye. The badge is in the style of the original Austin-Healey one. This is almost the first car to wear the Healey name alone since 1953, or thereabouts . . .

The cast-alloy wheels are a classic design in their own right; still 13in in diameter, although the rims and tyres are a trifle wider than they used to be on a Frog-eye Sprite.

If it can be called a replicar, it is a very authentic one. The headlamps and the wheels may not be as the original, but neither are out of place on the modern-day look-alike. Even the bonnet handle is there – although not actually required!

The boot badge with the arrow is modelled on the original Sprite badge but, like the grille badge, simply reads Frogeye.

Under the bonnet, things become more obvious, although it is still an A-series engine. There is an alternator, and an up-to-date cooling system.

Converted Spridgets

There used to be a fashion for converting Spridgets. There was the Lenham coupe which was a complete fibreglass rear body: a Kamm-tailed fastback design which could be fitted to any Spridget once you had snipped away most of the original rear end. Lenham also offered a front-hinged one-piece bonnet. Lenham styling was perhaps a trifle awkward in places, and the resulting car did not look quite so much like an original Sprite Le Mans works racing car as some people liked to think.

Then there was the Arkley which relied on fibreglass front and rear ends to transform the looks of the Spridget. It certainly succeeded, yet the appearance of the finished car was an uneasy mixture of Frog-eye Sprite and TF Midget, with a hint of Lotus Seven thrown in for good measure. The Lenham, the Arkley and others of that ilk are best regarded simply as fun cars, not to be taken entirely seriously. Such conversions were certainly one way to utilize the mechanical components of an ageing Spridget which might otherwise have gone to the breaker's yard with terminal corrosion. After all, it is not that long ago that Spridgets were considered expendable.

Apart from the wholesale and rather drastic approach of re-bodying, very many Spridgets display a degree of unoriginality, reflecting the tastes and requirements of individual owners. Especially on the later cars, some form of mild customizing seems to be the rule rather than the exception. In a way this is rather nice, because it proves that Spridgets are still being used and enjoyed rather than being put on pedestals. However, in general the trend now seems to be towards keeping cars in their original condition, so the best advice that I can give to anyone planning to modify a Spridget – or any other classic car – is to think very carefully before you do anything. Also, try not to carry out any modification which would make it difficult or impossible to bring the car back to original specification, should you change your mind at a later date, or should you sell the car to someone with a different approach.

FROG-EYE, WITHOUT TEARS

A side-effect of the booming classic car interest is that there is a growing demand for what may loosely be called 'replicars' – cars which look like the rare and sought-after originals, but which use modern mechanicals and are therefore expected to be more reliable and easy to live with. The American designer Brooks Stevens certainly started something with his first Mercedes-Benz lookalike, the 1964 Excalibur . . . In Britain, a similar trend began with the Panther J.72 based on the design of the SS Jaguar 100. This has been followed by a host of others, and it was inevitable that sooner or later, the Frog-eye Sprite would attract similar attention.

The man behind the re-born Frog-eye is Keith Brading of Ryde in the Isle of Wight. A long-standing enthusiast for the Frog-eye, he finally decided that rusting steel bodies and unreliable old mechanicals were not for him, and in 1985 started to develop a modern-day version of the car, giving it the name of 'Healey Frogeye'. Although the Healey Frogeye looks exactly like an original Sprite Mark I, it is a very different car. It sports a separate chassis designed by John Ackroyd (the designer of Richard Noble's Thrust II record car). The body is made from fibreglass, with a front-hinged bonnet. The engine is the later 1,275cc version of BMC's A-series, although Brading has his eye on a 1.6-litre Ford Sierra fuel-injected engine and a five-speed gearbox from the same source. Brading may also incorporate an independent rear-suspension set-up borrowed from the ubiquitous Ford in future cars. And the new Frogeye incorporates sundry other bits and pieces from a variety of present-day cars.

New Frogeyes for Old . . .

At first-glance, it is difficult to tell the difference between an original Sprite Mark I and Brading's Frogeye. The new car even keeps the bonnet handle below the radiator grille of the original, although with a front-hinged bonnet it serves no practical purpose! But the old round badge with the Austin coat of arms is missing, replaced by a winged badge on the grille surround bearing the words 'Healey Frogeye'. Keith Brading is particularly pleased that he obtained formal approval from Donald Healey (shortly before the latter's death in 1988) to use the Healey name and original badge on the car.

Then the new Frogeye runs on cast-alloy wheels, although chrome wire wheels can be specified. Inside, the facia is an almost exact replica of the original but with a few extra switches. A smaller diameter wood-rim steering-wheel is fitted and, because of the backbone chassis, the transmission tunnel is significantly more bulky. The characteristic gear-lever turret of the original has gone.

On the road, the 1991 version of the Frogeye is not unlike the original, but much improved according to people who have tried both. The performance is superior to the 948cc Sprite Mark I and is, in fact, very comparable to the 1,275cc-engined Sprite Mark IV or Midget Mark III. To cope with the extra power and present-day traffic, the new Frogeye has front disc brakes. The rear suspension uses rubber in torsion, the live axle is located by radius arms and there are telescopic shock absorbers in place of the original lever-arm dampers. The ride of the new car is perhaps the most dramatic improvement.

Keith Brading and his small team build the new Frogeyes virtually by hand. It is in many ways a much better conceived and better built car than the originals were. It is certainly a quality product, and there is no sign of any corners being cut. Brading likes to demonstrate how strong the fibreglass body is by jumping up and down on one. Apart from Donald Healey approving the car, Geoffrey Healey now acts as a consultant to Brading's Frogeye Car Company. Perhaps we shall see some of the improvements that the Healeys could never get BMC to approve for production in the 1960s, brought back for the new car thirty years later.

. . . at a Price

There is inevitably one snag. To get a fully-built new Frogeye will cost between £12,000 and £14,000. This frankly does not compare favourably with the cost of a new Mazda or Toyota, and is, broadly speaking, almost twice the 1958 price translated into modern money. It is also rather more than the value of a condition one restored or original car.

However, it is possible for you to buy what Brading calls a 'restoration assembly' for less than £4,000. This consists of a new chassis, complete glassfibre body, and the rear axle and suspension. All the customer has to do is to strip out a redundant rusted-out Spridget (any variety will do) and transfer the bits to the new body/chassis assembly. Every one of the new Frogeyes, whether supplied by Brading or re-built by customers from one of the assemblies, incorporates the old front-suspension cross-member and front chassis rails from an original car. So, although 90 per cent of the Brading-built cars are made up from new parts, this means that a new Frogeye can still assume the chassis number and identity of the original donor car. It avoids paying car tax and fitting Q-prefix number-plates, but may make life awkward for historians in the years to come!

AND FOR THE FUTURE?

The 1990s look set to become the green decade. There is a possibility that this will sooner or later also affect the classic car movement. It has already been decided to

The original Frog-eye design is as fresh and cheeky as ever, even after more than thirty years.

One of the very sensible things about the new Frogeye is that finally, here is a Sprite/Midget where you can get at the battery! Ironically, with modern batteries you do not need to attend to it as often as you used to.

And of course, with the forward-hinging bonnet everything is so much more accessible. Without full inner wing valances, the engine is unlikely to stay quite as clean as this for a long time.

There is not a great deal to give the game away even in the rear view; we will have to take a closer look in detail to spot the differences between the original and the modern Frog-eye.

The plaque on the dashboard bears the signature of Geoffrey Healey, signifying his support for, and approval of, Keith Brading's new Frogeye.

A wood-rim steering-wheel was and is a common accessory also on the original Frog-eye Sprites. These instruments are from the later chrome-bumper Spridgets, and the crackle-finish dashboard is also reminiscent of the later cars.

introduce emissions tests as part of the MoT test for older cars, with specific limits being set for all cars made on or after 1 August 1975 (although the limits are not unrealistic, and most classic cars should easily pass the test unless there is something wrong). Similarly, we are already being encouraged to use lead-free petrol, which has been the norm in the USA for more than a decade. It should be possible to adapt all Spridgets, whether with A-series engines or with the Triumph 1500 engine, to use lead-free petrol, even if this means fitting a new cylinder head with specially hardened valve seats.

There is always the possibility that oil prices may be substantially increased. The Spridgets are luckily very economical, and most models can return 40mpg (1,400km/100l) or more driven with a bit of care. Such economy is excellent for a 1960s or 1970s sports car, bearing in mind that the Spridgets are almost totally non-aerodynamic, although their small frontal area and low weight are a great help.

It is still an open question whether we shall see retrospective technical legislation brought in. We have already seen one example of this, when some years ago it became mandatory to use front seat-belts in all post-1964 cars. This posed no problem for Spridget owners, as seat-belt mounting points were built into the structure of all Spridgets from 1961 onwards. However, we may eventually see a complete ban on trafficators (never fitted to Spridgets, of course), and there could be proposals to fit hazard warning lights, rear fog guard lamps or even high-level brake lights to older vehicles. Alternatively, the Ministry of Transport may follow the German example by introducing mandatory noise levels, or become more concerned that vehicles actually adhere to original manufacturers' specifications – a sort of retrospective type approval system.

EEC Influence?

Some pessimists fear that the EEC will eventually force Westminster to adopt stricter legislation regarding the construction and use of motor vehicles, covering also older vehicles, including classic cars. The Federation of British Historic Vehicle Clubs has retained an observer and lobbyist in Bruxelles to keep an eye out for any proposals that may affect the use of classic vehicles. However, while Britain certainly has the largest classic car movement in any European country, there are also sizeable groups of enthusiasts in Germany, France, Italy and many other countries. The possibility exists for keeping in touch with enthusiasts in other European countries through the International Federation for Historic Vehicles (FIVA).

The technical requirements for older vehicles differ greatly from one country to the next, but it is important to realize that no country has banned or restricted the use of classic cars. Indeed, if the use of classic vehicles is ever restricted, it may perversely come about as a result of increasing values, which could make it difficult to obtain insurance cover for road use at a reasonable premium: like present-day agreed value policies stipulating a limited annual mileage, only more so ... Long may the Spridgets remain at their present affordable values!

For the time being, the idea of using a classic car is a fundamentally attractive and practical proposition for many enthusiasts, and the Spridgets are as attractive and practical as most. There is a wide choice of Spridgets on the market at any time, ranging in 1991 terms from a few hundred pounds for a down-at-heel Midget 1500 restoration project, to ten times as much (or more) for a *concours* Sprite Mark I – or even more for one of Keith Brading's Frogeyes!

12 Buying, Restoring and Maintaining

You may have bought and read this book because you are already a committed Spridget enthusiast, with one or more of these cars in your garage, front garden or at the kerb. Or, if not, you may have decided on the basis of what you have read so far that a Spridget is just the car for you, and you are about to rush out and spend your hard-earned cash on one. You probably have a budget of some sort, and it should not be too difficult to find a number of cars within your price bracket.

Look in the classified sections of the specialized classic car magazines, the classic car section of the *Exchange & Mart* or similar papers, but Spridgets may also appear in your local paper. If you are looking for a car, it is always a good idea to join the appropriate club – in this case the Austin-Healey Club or one of the MG clubs. In this way, you can check any cars that may be advertised for sale in club magazines or newsletters, and you can also go to the local meetings in your area, getting to know other local owners and enthusiasts.

VALUES AND PRICES

Relatively speaking, Spridgets are at the lower end of the classic car market, as you will soon find out by checking their values in one of the price guides which appear regularly in many classic car magazines. Do bear in mind that these guides are just that; they provide guide-lines to approximate values for cars depending on condition, based on the compilers' knowledge of the market and current market trends.

Cars actually offered for sale may carry asking prices very different from what you thought they should be. However, with the exception of the very best Mark I Sprites, Spridgets are generally very affordable. This means that most cars are likely to be offered for sale privately, rather than by traders, and it is relatively unusual to find Spridgets at the high-class London auctions, although they may turn up at the more modest sales held by provincial auction houses.

Because of the plentiful supply in the UK and the relatively low values, few Spridgets have been brought back from the USA, and although some Frog-eye Sprites have returned to the UK, they have been far outnumbered by Big Healeys, MGs and Triumphs. As the cost of conversion to right-hand drive is proportionally quite high for a Spridget, most of the ex-US cars have probably gone straight on to the European market.

Once you have established how much you can afford to spend and what sort of Spridget is within your reach, you should try to look at a number of cars, and if you do not know much about car mechanics in general and Spridgets in particular, try to enlist the help of a fellow club member who can hopefully offer disinterested and expert advice.

RUST PROBLEMS

The very biggest problem with Spridgets (except Mr Brading's fibreglass clones!) is

It was, and is, very common for enthusiastic owners to add a few extra instruments to the Frog-eye dashboard.

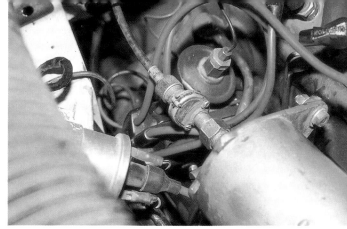

One area which is often the cause of trouble: the mechanical rev counter driven off the back of the dynamo, used from 1958 until 1962.

The only way to make sure you really turned off the heater is by closing the water-valve with the brass tap at the back of the cylinder head.

The fresh-air intake trunking on the left leads to the fan, which is then linked to the heat exchange matrix in the black box behind the engine.

The radio, loud speaker and steering-wheel cover are the major deviations from originality in this interior.

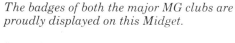

The badges of both the major MG clubs are proudly displayed on this Midget.

Technical literature such as this driver's handbook is useful reading. Original books are much prized, but reprints are available for most models.

It is always a pleasure to inspect a nicely-prepared and well-cleaned engine compartment. A little bit of customizing, such as this non-standard rocker cover, is perfectly legitimate.

It would take a brave man to tackle a Spridget found in this condition, but nothing is impossible! However, a car such as this could well need an all-new bodyshell, and may be best approached as a source of parts.

Even a car which looks undamaged on top can be far gone below. Potential restoration costs should be evaluated carefully, bearing in mind the plentiful availability of Spridgets and the modest values these cars attract.

that they rust. Rust is not an insuperable problem, but it may cost a lot of money to put right, in new body panels as well as labour. It is not unknown for well-used Spridgets to need a completely new floor, for instance. Adding this to the cost of new sills, door bottoms, front and rear wings, possibly bonnet, rear bulkhead and boot floor, you may decide to leave that particular car alone, or you may decide that what you really need is an all-new bodyshell.

These are now available, thanks to British Motor Heritage who introduced the new MGB roadster bodyshell in 1988, and in 1990 followed this up with the MGB GT shell. The first Heritage Spridget bodyshell was launched in April 1991. The Heritage Spridget body comes complete with wings, doors, bonnet and boot-lid, but it is also available in basic form, without these panels. It is based on the 1964–1974 period chrome-bumper cars, either of the square-arch or the round-arch variety, and is equally suitable for a Sprite as for a Midget.

There may well be a follow-up in the shape of a new shell for the rubber-bumper Midget 1500. However, because of the difference in the rear springs, the Heritage body is less suitable for the earlier models with quarter-elliptic springs. As the special tooling for the unique Frog-eye panels is no longer in existence, it would be more problematical for Heritage to make a completely new bodyshell for the Sprite Mark I.

BODYSHELLS

The theory is simple. Take one rusted-out donor Spridget, strip all the mechanical and trim parts, and transfer these to your new shell. In practice, it does require a fair degree of expertise. A keen do-it-yourself restorer can certainly tackle it at home, but it could be a long job, and it is likely that you will want to renovate or renew many other parts as you go along. Based on the experience with the

MGB bodyshell over a two-year period, it seems probable that most Spridget shells will be sold to the professional classic car restorers who will then be able to offer rebuilt Spridgets, in the same way that a number of firms are now offering re-built MGBs.

The Heritage bodyshells are not sold direct from the Heritage factory at Faringdon, but are available to order from any of the approved Heritage specialists, many of whom cater for Spridgets. They can be identified by their use of the Heritage logo in their advertising. Each of these outlets will be able to supply full information on the Heritage bodyshells, or the range of Spridget body panels also supplied by the British Motor Heritage.

THE MECHANICALS

The body is always the biggest problem on a Spridget. It proves difficult to restore and very difficult to prevent from rusting again, especially if you use the car all year round. (If global warming means less salt on roads in winter, that at least will be good news!) By contrast the mechanicals are simple and straightforward. BMC A-series engines are generally robust and reliable, although the 1,098cc engine of 1962–1964 (type 10CG) is more fragile than the rest because of its small main bearings. However, very many Spridgets have acquired replacement engines over the years, and if you are concerned that a car may have had a replacement engine, please refer to Appendix 1 of this book giving details of all the original engine prefixes, model by model and year by year.

In the past, a tired Spridget engine would very often be replaced by a Morris Minor 1000 or Austin A40 Farina engine which are both of the same basic design. Typically, many such engines would then be fitted with the manifolds and carburettors from the original Spridget engine, and can be difficult to spot unless you check the engine number. The 1,500cc Triumph engine found in the later rubber-bumper Midget has a reputation of being not quite so robust as the A-series, particularly as regards the bottom end. Many Midget 1500s have acquired different replacement engines, some from Spitfires, some from Toledos or Dolomites, possibly even from Heralds!

Gearboxes

As far as gearboxes are concerned, the most important point is that the early gearboxes (before the introduction of baulk-ring synchromesh) have rather weak second-gear synchromesh. First gear is not synchronized at all, which may take a bit of getting used to for anyone more accustomed to modern gearboxes. The Frog-eye Sprite gearbox is considered to be somewhat of a weak point of this model, and should not be abused. The rear axle is likely to be noisy but is typical of many BMC designs in that the noise is usually not ominous.

Early cars with quarter-elliptic springs usually emit any number of squeaks from the radius-arm rubbers. Some owners seem to become quite attached to their individual squeaks, rattles and groans ... The radius arms have often rusted and need replacing. Other points to look out for are the king pins which will typically need renewal, and sometimes the lower wishbones as well, if the lower trunnions have worn badly. The lever-arm dampers will almost certainly need rebuilding or replacing.

PAINT, TRIM AND HOOD

What colour you paint your car is an entirely personal choice, but if you are concerned about originality yet can't abide the colour your car originally was (Primrose Yellow or Deep Pink are not everybody's cup of tea) the most legitimate solution would be to pick another paint colour correct for the model and year in question. You will also make life much simpler for yourself if you pick a colour which is still correct for your trim colour – unless you are prepared to have the car retrimmed to match.

As far as type of paint is concerned, originally the Spridgets were finished in straightforward ordinary synthetic paint (as opposed to cellulose), but for restoration purposes go for the best that modern paint technology can offer. Virtually all of the Spridget colours are still recognized by paint manufacturers and can be mixed or reformulated from the paint supplier's code number.

If you need to re-trim, the many trim kits available make this a fairly straightforward matter. No Spridget ever had leather upholstery, not even as an option, so while you can retrim in leather, it is strictly speaking not original.

The rubber mats used on the Frogeye Sprite and on the 1961–1962 period Spridgets are rather a problem, and because of unavailability of reproduction rubber mats, many of these cars have been fitted with carpets during restoration. All trim parts were usually the same colour, and the carpets (or rubber mats) matched the trim colour.

Hoods need replacing sooner or later, and it would be very unusual if a Spridget had not had one or more hood replacements during its career. Hoods and tonneau covers are easily available, at least in black, which is the predominant hood colour for most Spridgets. You might have to ferret around a bit to find the exact colour match if you have one of the early 1960s cars which should have a coloured hood. Of all the trim and hood colours, Hazelnut is by far the rarest.

PARTS INTERCHANGEABILITY

People used to say that it was simple to get parts for the Spridgets because they had so

Many such cars are now being broken up for spares, which help to keep other and better examples on the road.

For long-term peace of mind, it is not a bad idea to have a few extra bits and pieces stashed away somewhere – attic, garage, garden shed – you never know what may come in handy!

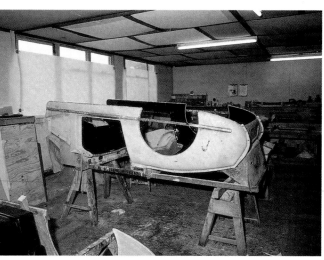

The secret behind the perfect looks of the new Frogeye is the fibreglass body, which provides a strong yet very light shell, and completely avoids rust problems.

This car is well on the way to completion, with the body mounted on the chassis. Colour is, of course, to the customer's choice.

The Frogeye is given extra backbone by this chassis, which incorporates the front chassis legs from an original donor car.

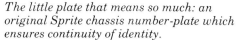

The little plate that means so much: an original Sprite chassis number-plate which ensures continuity of identity.

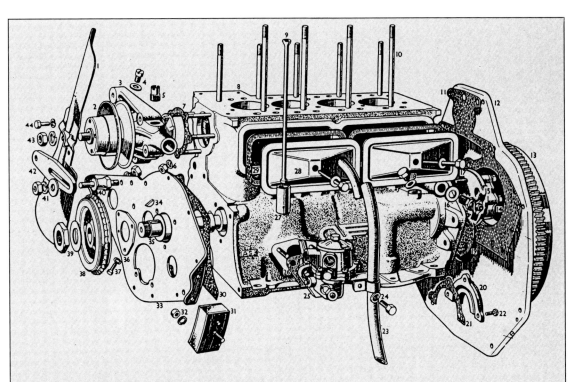

Cylinder block and crankcase of the Frog-eye engine.

1	Fan blade	23	Crankcase vent pipe
2	Water pump pulley	24	Setscrew and washer
3	Water pump	25	Petrol pump
4	Water pump screwed plug and washer	26	Petrol pump joint washer
5	Water pump by-pass tube	27	Tappet
6	Nut and washer for water pump stud	28	Cylinder side cover, front
7	Water pump joint washer	29	Joint washer for side cover
8	Cylinder block	30	Front mounting plate joint washer
9	Push rod	31	Rubber mounting
10	Cylinder head studs in block	32	Nut and washer for rubber mounting
11	Rear mounting plate joint washer	33	Engine front mounting plate
12	Rear mounting plate	34	Woodruff key
13	Flywheel and starter ring	35	Camshaft
14	Oil pump	36	Camshaft locating plate
15	Cylinder block drain tap	37	Setscrew and shakeproof washer
16	Washer for drain tap	38	Camshaft gear and tensioner rings
17	Setscrew and washer for side cover	39	Nut and lockwasher
18	Oil priming plug and joint washer	40	Pillar for adjusting link
19	Oil pump joint washer	41	Nut and washers for pulley
20	Crankcase rear cover	42	Dynamo adjusting link
21	Joint washer for rear cover	43	Nut and washer for pulley
22	Rear cover setscrew	44	Setscrew and washer for fan blade

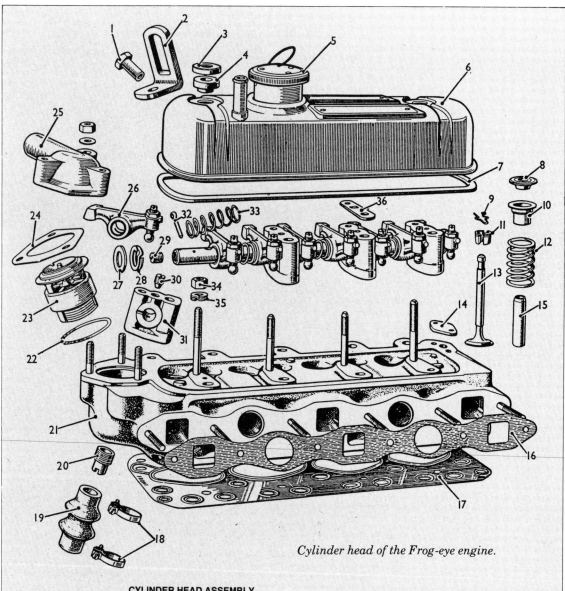

Cylinder head of the Frog-eye engine.

CYLINDER HEAD ASSEMBLY

1 Valve rocker cover cap nut
2 Engine sling bracket
3 Cup washer
4 Ruber bush
5 Oil filler cap
6 Valve rocker cover
7 Rocker cover joint washer
8 Valve spring cup
9 Valve cotter circlip
10 Valve oil seal retainer
11 Valve cotters
12 Valve spring
13 Valve
14 Cover plate
15 Valve guide
16 Joint washer
17 Gasket
18 Hose clips

19 By-pass hose
20 By-pass tube
21 Cylinder head
22 Thermostat joint washer
23 Thermostat
24 Water outlet elbow joint washer
25 Water outlet elbow
26 Rocker
27 Plain washer
28 Spring washer
29 Rocker shaft plug
30 Locating grub screw
31 Rocker shaft pedestal
32 Split pin
33 Rocker spacing spring
34 Rocker bracket nut
35 Rocker bracket washer
36 Rocker bracket plate

much in common with the BMC and BL bread-and-butter family cars. This was true as long as there was a steady demand for parts for a large stock of Morris Minors, Austin A35s and A40s, and the like. As the years have gone by, the boot is increasingly on the other foot, and now it is as likely to be the Austin or Morris saloon car owner who benefits from the greater availability of spare parts for the Spridgets.

Of the BMC family cars of the 1960s, only the Morris Minor and the Mini are as well catered for by parts specialists as the sports car models. Typically, anyone bent on improving one of the small Austin or Morris saloons will begin by raiding the Spridget parts bin.

Much of the ground has already been covered in earlier chapters, but to briefly sum up, the following are those areas where parts communality is most important and may work to the benefit of either the Spridget owner, or the saloon owner:

- 948cc engine (Sprite Mark I/II 1958–1962; Midget Mark I) shared with Austin A35, Austin A40 Mark I, Morris Minor 1000 (1956–1962).
- 1,098cc engine (Sprite Mark II/III and Midget Mark I/II, 1962–1966) shared with Austin A40 Mark II, some Austin A35 vans, Morris Minor 1000 (1962–1971); many parts also common to BMC 1100s and even later front-wheel drive cars.
- 1,275cc engine (Sprite Mark IV, Midget Mark III) shared with Morris Marina 1300; many parts also common to BMC 1300s and Allegro 1300.
- 1,500cc engine (Midget 1500) shared with Triumph Spitfire, Triumph 1500 (rear-wheel drive) and Toledo/Dolomite range; very similar to Herald/Spitfire/Toledo 1,300cc models.
- Gearboxes, 1958–1974: basically same design as Austin A35/A40/Morris Minor of the same year.
- All-synchro gearbox, Midget 1500 (1974–

1979): Morris Marina (and very similar to many rear-wheel drive Triumphs).
- Rear axle: final drive with different (higher) ratio and different axle casing on quarter-elliptic cars (1958–1962). Otherwise, basically same BMC design as found on small Austin and Morris saloons of the period.
- Front suspension: Austin A35/A40 models.
- Steering rack (1958–1974): Morris Minor 1000.

Equally important is the interchangeability of parts between the various Sprite and Midget models, but the specialist spare parts suppliers will be extremely well clued up on this. They also often publish extensive lists of parts which they have available. Unipart ceased publishing parts lists in book format many years ago, but the parts lists for Spridgets from 1964 onwards (all models from Sprite Mark III and Midget Mark II onwards) are still available in microfiche format, and should still be available in the parts department of Rover Car dealers, together with parts lists for the Morris Minor 1000 and Austin A40 Farina Mark II.

HINTS AND TIPS

If you are looking at Spridgets with a view to buying a car, or even if you own one, check that the details on the vehicle registration document actually match the chassis (car) number and engine number you find on the car itself. Many people never bother to look. In fact, probably more than one in ten registration documents have errors on them, either made when the car was first registered or as a result of careless transcription later on. Nor are all engine changes entered on the car's documents. Some cars may have been registered with the body number as the 'chassis number', and so on.

Some chassis number-plates may have

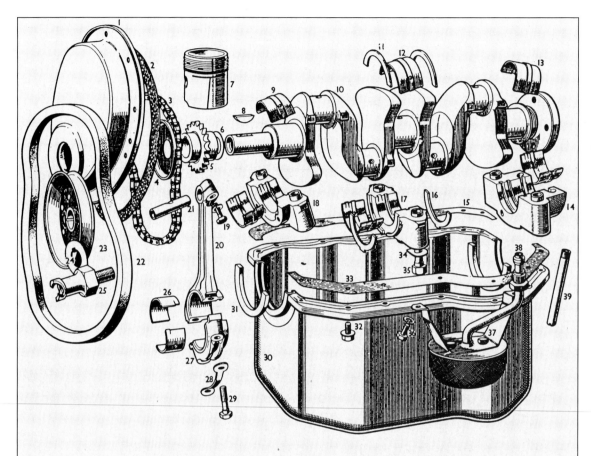

Crankshaft and sump of the Frog-eye engine.

THE CRANKSHAFT AND SUMP ASSEMBLY

1	Engine front cover	21	Gudgeon pin
2	Joint washer for cover	22	Vee-belt for fan and pulley
3	Timing chain	23	Crankshaft pulley
4	Crankshaft oil thrower	24	Lockwasher
5	Crankshaft gear	25	Starting nut
6	Packing washers	26	Connecting rod half bearing
7	Piston	27	Connecting rod cap
8	Woodruff key	28	Lockwasher
9	Front main half bearing	29	Setscrew for connecting rod
10	Crankshaft	30	Oil sump
11	Thrust washer, upper	31	Cork sealing washer
12	Centre main half bearing	32	Setscrew and captive washer
13	Rear main half bearing	33	Oil sump joint washer, left
14	Rear main bearing cap and dowels	34	Main bearing cap lockwasher
15	Oil sump joint washer, right	35	Setscrew for main bearing cap
16	Thrust washer, lower	36	Setscrew and shakeproof washer for strainer and bracket
17	Centre main bearing cap and dowels	37	Oil strainer
18	Front main bearing cap and dowels	38	Suction pipe
19	Clamping screw and washer for (20)	39	Drain pipe for rear main bearing cap
20	Connecting rod, less cap		

The modest premises of the Frogeye Car Company. The atmosphere inside is reminiscent of the good old days at Warwick or Abingdon.

The engine is installed once chassis and body have been successfully married.

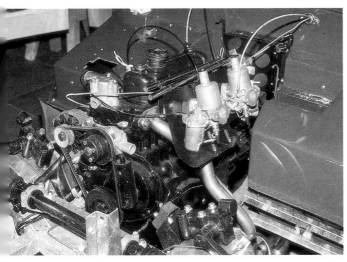

More work in progress. This particular car would appear to use one of the late Midget 1,275cc engines of the 1972–1974 period. Of course, the engine does not have to come from an original Spridget; A-series engines of humbler origin can always be brought up to the desired specification.

The front disc brakes are one of those improvements that help to make the Frogeye more suitable for modern driving conditions.

It is evident throughout that the new Frogeye are prepared to a very high standard.

A respect for the original design, coupled with intelligent and worthwhile improvements, the use of quality materials and components put together with more than usual care, all help to make the Frogeye a very special car.

been lost during restoration (reproductions are now available), or sometimes for nefarious purposes. If the numbers on the documents are significantly different to those found on the car, be wary! If the car has been off the road for so long that it has never been registered on the DVLA computer at Swansea, it may still be possible to have the original registration mark re-issued under the new rules introduced in 1990, but typically, only if the original log book is available. If it is not, it is normally so difficult to prove that the number-plate on the car is actually the right one that it is not worth bothering. If the year of manufacture can be established, a car can always be re-registered under a new 'age-related' number, and these are also available for re-imported cars which have to be registered in the UK for the first time.

Read Up!

To aid any restoration, maintenance or service work, the do-it-yourself enthusiast would do well to get hold of suitable technical literature. Reprints have been made of most of the relevant original Spridget workshop manuals, and these can be obtained from the spares suppliers, the clubs, or specialist bookshops. However, do bear in mind that the original factory publications were written for professional motor mechanics and tend to use 'mechanic's short-hand'.

The private amateur is often better served by an owner's workshop manual, such as those published by Haynes, which tend to go into rather more detail. Those who *must* have original publications, however dog-eared, can do no better than rummage around at autojumbles – there are likely to be several literature stalls at the bigger events – and this is also the best source for original sales leaflets, drivers' handbooks and the like. There are some books which deal especially with the actual restoration, and these are likely to be even more useful than the original workshop manuals, as they have been written and illustrated by experts who have successfully completed several restoration projects, from wreck to *concours*.

Do remember that even if you do most of the work yourself, there is always a cost involved in restoration: parts, or those jobs which simply cannot be done at home in the garage, such as re-chroming. Like the Channel tunnel, most restoration projects end up costing a lot more than you originally bargained for. The point of this is that it is very easy to spend a lot more money on restoration than the car will be worth when it is finished. Hence those frequently-encountered advertisements for cars which 'only need a small amount of work to finish . . . bills for £x,000' and an asking price of rather less than £x,000.

The Spridgets mostly fall into the category of cars which end up being worth less than the total cost of restoration. The Frog-eye Sprite Mark I is possibly the only exception, and even for this car you cannot always expect to re-coup your investment. Classic car restoration is not a case of doing a quick job and making a quick buck. Professional restoration is as expensive as it is because when you are in business, on your own or employing other people, you have to cover your costs and charge by the hour. However, if you plan to keep, love and cherish your Spridget for ever after, don't worry about the sordid economics. For long-term peace of mind, it is probably better to spend a little bit over the odds and end up with a first-class result.

AND AFTER . . .

One day, it is all finished. The last bit has been screwed back on, and off you go in your gleaming as-new Spridget to the nearest garage, returning with a fresh MoT test certificate. The problem is, what do you do next? Quite a surprising number of people promptly lose interest in a car once it has been restored and look around for a new challenge. Some plump for the same type of car, hoping perhaps that the next job will be easier now that they have gained hard-won expertise; others tend to trade up, literally to a bigger car, or to an older vehicle.

Assuming, however, that you *do* keep your Spridget, you will obviously want to show it off. Even if you are not interested in the hard-core *concours* scene, there are plenty of local and national club meets, other classic car events or shows to take the car to. Many Spridget owners use their car very regularly in almost all conditions; others keep them as second cars and only do a limited mileage in fine weather.

Whatever use you make of the car, there will always be some routine servicing or maintenance work to be undertaken. Do not skimp on this. Remember that one reason why the car needed a total restoration in the first place was that some nameless owner in the past just could not be bothered. This is where you should follow the maker's original instructions almost to the letter, and even if you only do a very limited mileage, it is a wise precaution to undertake at least one annual service.

Maintain and Protect

Although it may sound like very basic advice, do keep the car clean. Dirt and mud trap water, which inevitably leads to corrosion. Tedious and difficult though it may be, the underside of the car is almost the most important part to clean. If you do not keep the engine bay clean, it very soon starts to look gungy, and it is easier to spot oil leaks on a clean engine than on a dirty one. Wire wheels are inevitably much more difficult to clean than disc wheels or Rostyle wheels, but they are worth taking trouble over.

Spridget interiors are fairly simple to keep tidy, thanks to the Vynide or Ambla upholstery. On the Frog-eye and other early cars with rubber mats, you could almost hose the inside down – except for the problem of drainage!

Each individual Spridget owner will face his or her particular problems, either during restoration or at some other time. Therefore, the brief remarks in this chapter can only be a general guide to the pleasures and pitfalls of Spridget ownership. To return to a point which I made earlier on, perhaps the best piece of advice to any classic car owner is to join the appropriate club, get to know fellow owners and enthusiasts and never be afraid to ask questions. A problem shared is often a problem solved. Whatever use you make of your Spridget, do look after it – and I hope you will enjoy owning and using one of these cars. It is one of the best of the classic British sports cars.

13 Identifying Your Spridget

The most important point of identification of a Sprite or Midget is the chassis number (which we now have to become used to calling the VIN, or Vehicle Identification Number). This is the number that should be found on your Log Book or Vehicle Registration Document (or, in the USA, the Title Document). The same number should also be stamped on the Manufacturer's Plate which is attached to the side of the engine compartment. (For instance, on a Frog-eye it will be found on the inner wing valance, just by the air filters.)

The plate will carry the name of the manufacturer – either 'Austin Motor Company Limited' or 'The MG Car Company Limited', in later years changed to 'Austin-Morris Group – British Leyland (UK) Limited' and, finally, possibly to 'BL Cars Limited'. On this plate, the chassis number is called the 'car number'. Do not be confused, however, the 'car number' *is* the 'chassis number'. The car or chassis number was not normally stamped in the bodyshell, except on later export models, especially to North America.

PREFIXES

The car/chassis number has a prefix which identifies the actual model, and for the different models of Sprite and Midget, refer to the prefixes listed in the table below.

It is really quite confusing that the 'Mark' numbers are always one out of step! These prefixes obviously mean something. BMC had a very well thought out chassis-number prefix system, based originally on Austin practice and used on all their products from 1959, until well into the Leyland era. In these prefixes, the first letter identifies the make of car, which may be either H for Austin-Healey, G for MG, or A for Austin – but please note that the Frog-eye Sprite never had the initial letter H.

The second letter in a Spridget prefix (which, in case of the Frog-eye is the *first* letter!) is always A, which tells us that these are small cars with engines originally of less than 1,200cc; if you like, A-series engines. Then, there is the letter N, which indicates

Production period	Sprite	Midget
1958–1961	Mark I: AN5	
1961–1962	Mark II, 948cc: H-AN6	Mark I, 948cc: G-AN1
1962–1964	Mark II, 1,098cc: H-AN7	Mark I, 1,098cc: G-AN2
1964–1966	Mark III: H-AN8	Mark II: G-AN3
1966–1969	Mark IV: H-AN9	Mark III: G-AN4
1969–1970	Mark IV: H-AN10	Mark III: G-AN5
1971	Austin Sprite: A-AN10	Mark III: G-AN5
1971–1974		Mark III: G-AN5
1974–1979		1500: G-AN6

that all these cars had open two-seater body-work. The final number simply indicates the series of the model, and was changed when-ever a major modification or a re-design was introduced.

These prefix codes would be followed by a letter L if the car in question was fitted with left-hand drive, but in 1967 when it became necessary to introduce substantially differ-ent models for the North American market, North American specification cars were from then onwards identified by the letter U rather than an L.

SUFFIXES

Another change introduced by BMC during the 1960s and which seems to apply to Spridgets from 1967 onwards, is that the chassis number was given a suffix letter to indicate in which factory the car had been built. On most Spridgets this suffix letter was G, indicating that they were made in the MG factory at Abingdon, but on those few Spridgets which were assembled in the Mor-ris factory at Cowley during 1967, the suffix letter should be M.

The actual car or chassis numbers were issued in three different series. The first series of numbers was used only for the Frog-eye or Mark I Sprite. This series of numbers ran from 501 to 50116. The Sprite Mark II to Mark IV models used the second series num-bers, from 101 to 87824; and the third series of numbers was used for all of the MG Midgets from 1961 to 1979. The Midget series of numbers also began with 101 and con-tinued to 229526.

From 1970 onwards, the practice was adopted of having a break or gap in the number series between each model year. Also from 1970 onwards, on North American ex-port models, an extra letter was added to the chassis-number prefix, indicating the model year. These model-year identification letters were as follows:

A	= 1970	F	= 1975
B	= 1971	G	= 1976
C	= 1972	H	= 1977
D	= 1973	J	= 1978
E	= 1974	L	= 1979

Therefore, a late North American specifica-tion MG Midget could have a chassis number such as G-AN6-UJ/200001-G, and a late home market car a number such as G-AN6/229526-G.

In the tables found in Appendix 1, the chassis number series for both Sprite and Midget models have been set out chronologi-cally year by year.

ENGINE NUMBERS

The other important number, which should also be found on your Log Book or Registra-tion Document, is the engine number. Again, BMC had a unified system of engine-number prefixes. These prefixes begin with a number which indicates the capacity of the engine, and which may be either 9 for 948cc, 10 for 1,098cc or 12 for 1,275cc. This number is followed by one or two letters indicating which make and model this engine belonged to; on a Spridget there is usually a C in the first position after the capacity-indicating number. These first characters together indi-cate the type and application of the engine.

The remaining letters in the engine-number prefix give an idea of the specifica-tion of the engine and transmission. A letter U indicates that there is a floor-mounted centre gearchange, but if the letters DA are found, we know that there is a close-ratio gearbox with a floor-mounted centre gear-change. Finally, there will be a letter H, or more rarely L, for either High or Low com-pression.

New Prefix System

Towards the end of the 1960s, BMC intro-

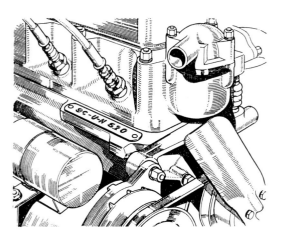

This is where you find the engine number and the car (chassis) number on a Frog-eye.

duced a new engine-number prefix system. These new prefixes were introduced on the MG Midget in late 1971 but were never found on any Sprites (as the Sprite had gone out of production by then). The new-style prefixes still had a number to start with, in this case 12 for the 1,275cc capacity, but next came the letter V (meaning 'vertical') on in-line engines for rear-wheel drive cars. After the V followed a three-figure code number which indicated the detailed specification of the engine, and thus also defined which model of car the engine applied to. Next came the letter F for two carburettors, or the letter Z for two carburettors with emissions control, and finally the letter H or L for high or low compression. By now, North American engines always had low compression.

Each type of engine had its own series of numbers, each series of numbers starting with 101. From 1961 to 1971, each series of engine numbers was shared between Sprites and Midgets, with the same engine number prefixes on both cars.

The Midget 1500 from 1974 to 1979 used a Triumph Spitfire engine so, of course, the engine prefix on this model also followed the Triumph system. These engines have a two-letter prefix which is FP; in the Triumph system, the first letter F is always indicative

of a Spitfire, but the Spitfire 1500 engine had the prefix FM. The Midget 1500 engine numbers were suffixed with an E (which simply shows that this is an Engine number), but North American specification engines had the suffix UE, or on Californian cars, UCE.

A complete list of all the different Spridget engine number prefixes is set out in Appendix 1. If you find an engine in a Spridget with a prefix which starts 8G, it does *not* mean that this is an 848cc MG engine; the 8G prefixes were used on BMC reconditioned replacement engines, later known as Gold Seal engines. These 8G prefixes are in fact the actual part numbers of the reconditioned units.

BODY NUMBERS

The third number which is usually worth looking at is the body number. This is simply the number of the body as a unit, and should not be confused with the chassis number, but unfortunately they often are! This happens particularly in case of the Frog-eye Sprite, where the Service Parts List claims that the body number is the number prefixed AN5 found on the left-hand front door pillar. The actual body number which is listed in the production records is prefixed BAE and is found on the *right*-hand front door pillar.

For some strange reason, many BMC cars seem to have two body numbers, of which usually only one is listed in the production records. On the Sprite Mark II and later models, the correct body number has the prefix ABL, while the MG Midget body numbers are prefixed GBE. These prefixes are found on all models until approximately 1967, but then North American specification cars began to have their own series of body numbers, and later on home market cars were also given new body numbers with different prefixes. For instance, the Midget 1500 body numbers were prefixed with GB47T on home market cars, and GU47T on North American cars. Here G obviously means MG, B or U means Britain or USA, 47 is the Midget's drawing office project number (as in ADO47), and T means Tourer.

A real red herring is the Commission Number, found on many BMC cars from approximately 1967 onwards. Again, the commission number should not be confused with the car/chassis number, and no one really knows why BMC issued these commission numbers when, very often, they never bothered to list them in the production records. Commission number prefixes start with a letter for the make of car, either G for MG or H for Austin-Healey, followed by the ADO (Amalgamated Drawing Office) number, which was 41 for the Sprite Mark II to Mark IV, and 47 for the Midget. There would then be a letter N for the open two-seater body.

Apart from the engine, other major components such as the gearbox and the rear axle also have individual numbers, but these numbers tend not to have any identifying prefixes, and they are not always listed in the production records anyway.

Summing up, the one really important number is the *car number* or *chassis number*, and if you find that the number on the plate under the bonnet does *not* match the number on your documentation, then there is a problem! The same applies if the plate with the car number is missing altogether . . . If you find that the engine-number prefix does not match any of the prefixes quoted in the list on page 218, then the engine is likely to have been changed for some kind of non-original engine, typically from an Austin A35 or A40 Farina, from a Morris Minor or from a Morris Marina; or, in case of the Midget 1500, from one of the numerous Triumphs using the same family of engines (Herald, Spitfire, Toledo, 1500 TC, or Dolomite 1300/1500).

The Clubs

The Austin-Healey Club was originally formed by BMC in the 1950s as a twin to the MG Car Club, and until 1968 operated from the Abingdon factory. When BLMC discontinued car club support, both the MG Car Club and the Austin-Healey Club had to rely on voluntary assistance. Although much smaller in the UK than the MG clubs, the Austin-Healey Club has continued to flourish.

Within the club is a register specially for the Sprite models. The club publishes a bi-monthly magazine, *Rev Counter*, and organizes a variety of rallies, *concours* and sporting events. In addition to the mainly UK-based club, there are a number of independent Austin-Healey clubs overseas, particularly in North America. Information on overseas clubs may also be obtained from the address of the UK club, which is:

The Austin-Healey Club
c/o Mrs Carol Marks
171 Coldharbour Road
Bristol BS6 7SX

Sprite Register; SAE to:
The White House
34 Main Street
Overseal
Burton-on-Trent DE12 5LG

Of the two main MG clubs, the MG Car Club is the oldest, as it was founded in 1930 (by, among others, John Thornley). It was run by the company until 1968, but has since become independent. The MG Car Club includes a register for 'Modern Midgets'. A monthly magazine, *Safety Fast*, is published, and of many club events the traditional Silverstone weekend in May is the largest, combining racing and *concours*.

The MG Car Club has a large number of centres and affiliated clubs overseas. In its diamond jubilee year of 1990, the club was finally able to achieve its long-cherished dream of returning to Abingdon, and now owns a property next door to the old MG factory. The address is:

The MG Car Club Ltd
Kimber House
Cemetery Road
PO Box 251
Abingdon
Oxfordshire OX14 1FF
UK
Tel: (0235) 555552

The MG Owners' Club was founded in 1973 and has grown to become one of the largest one-make car clubs in the world, with over 50,000 members. Most of these are resident in the UK, where the club has a large number of well-supported local groups. The club offers a particularly wide range of services which should be attractive to the Midget owner, such as an insurance scheme, a club shop, technical advice and reprinted literature, and even has its own workshop. The club publishes a monthly magazine, *Enjoying MG*, and a yearbook full of useful information, including addresses of many Midget service or parts specialists, who are part of the club's approval scheme. For further details, contact:

The MG Owners' Club
2/4 Station Road
Swavesey
Cambridgeshire CB4 5QZ
Tel: (0954) 31125.

Appendix 1

Austin-Healey Sprite Price Development (1958–1971)

(Total prices including Purchase Tax quoted to nearest whole Pound)

MODEL	DATE	BASIC	TOTAL	NOTES
Mark I	May 1958	£445	£669	Introduction of Mark I
Mark I	Apr 1959	£445	£631	Reduction of Purchase Tax
Mark II standard	May 1961	£452	£641	Introduction of Mark II
Mark II de-luxe	May 1961	£462	£656	
Mark II standard	Jul 1961	£452	£660	10 per cent surcharge on Purchase Tax
Mark II de-luxe	Jul 1961	£462	£675	
Mark II standard	Apr 1962	£452	£623	Reduction of Purchase Tax
Mark II de-luxe	Apr 1962	£462	£636	
Mark II 1,098cc	Oct 1962	£485	£668	Introduction of 1,098cc model
Mark II 1,098cc	Nov 1962	£485	£587	Reduction of Purchase Tax
Mark III	Mar 1964	£505	£611	Introduction of Mark III
Mark III	Sep 1964	£505	£612	Adjustment of Purchase Tax
Mark III	Jul 1966	£505	£622	Increase of Purchase Tax
Mark IV	Oct 1966	£545	£672	Introduction of Mark IV
Mark IV	Mar 1968	£545	£698	Increase of Purchase Tax
Mark IV	May 1968	£565	£724	Increase of basic price
Mark IV	Oct 1968	£577	£739	Increase of basic price
Mark IV	Nov 1968	£577	£756	Increase of Purchase Tax
Mark IV	Oct 1969	£625	£818	Increase of basic price
Mark IV	Mar 1970	£640	£838	Increase of basic price
Mark IV	Oct 1970	£692	£906	Increase of basic price
Austin Sprite	Jan 1971	£706	£924	Introduction of Austin Sprite, increase of basic price
Austin Sprite	Apr 1971	£741	£970	Increase of basic price
Austin Sprite	Jul 1971	£741	£928	Reduction of Purchase Tax, model discontinued

MG Midget Price Development (1961–1981)

(Total prices including Purchase Tax, or Car Tax and VAT, quoted to nearest whole Pound)

MODEL	DATE	BASIC	TOTAL	NOTES
Mark I 948cc	Jun 1961	£472	£670	Introduction of Mark I
Mark I 948cc	Jul 1961	£472	£689	10 per cent surcharge on Purchase Tax
Mark I 948cc	Apr 1962	£472	£650	Reduction of Purchase Tax
Mark I 1,098cc	Oct 1962	£495	£682	Introduction of 1,098cc model
Mark I 1,098cc	Nov 1962	£495	£599	Reduction of Purchase Tax
Mark II	Mar 1964	£515	£623	Introduction of Mark II
Mark II	Sep 1964	£515	£624	Adjustment of Purchase Tax
Mark II	Jul 1966	£515	£636	Increase of Purchase Tax
Mark III	Oct 1966	£555	£684	Introduction of Mark III
Mark III	Mar 1968	£555	£710	Increase of Purchase Tax
Mark III	May 1968	£575	£737	Increase of basic price
Mark III	Nov 1968	£575	£751	Increase of Purchase Tax
Mark III	Jan 1969	£587	£769	Increase of basic price
Mark III	Oct 1969	£625	£818	Increase of basic price
Mark III	Mar 1970	£640	£838	Increase of basic price
Mark III	Oct 1970	£692	£906	Increase of basic price
Mark III	Jan 1971	£706	£924	Increase of basic price
Mark III	Apr 1971	£741	£970	Increase of basic price
Mark III	Jul 1971	£741	£928	Reduction of Purchase Tax

(To simplify the table, individual price increases have been omitted from the following years, and only the price in each January quoted)

MODEL	DATE	BASIC	TOTAL	NOTES
Mark III	Jan 1972	£741	£928	No change
Mark III	Jan 1973	£829	£1,003	
Mark III	Jan 1974	£867	£1,033	Purchase Tax now replaced by Car Tax and VAT
Mark III	Oct 1974	£1,029	£1,204	Mark III discontinued
Midget 1500	Oct 1974	£1,155	£1,351	Introduction of Midget 1500
Midget 1500	Jan 1975	£1,155	£1,351	No change
Midget 1500	Jan 1976	£1,472	£1,722	No change
Midget 1500	Jan 1977	£1,761	£2,060	No change
Midget 1500	Jan 1978	£1,898	£2,221	No change
Midget 1500	Jan 1979	n/a	£2,802	No change
Midget 1500	Jan 1980	n/a	£3,604	Production stopped Nov 1979
Midget 1500	Jan 1981	n/a	£3,821	Final list price quoted

'Eternal Rivals...'

(Comparison of annual production figures for Sprite, Midget and Triumph Spitfire – including production of CKD cars for assembly abroad, but excluding the Sprite-based Innocentis)

YEAR	SPRITE	MIDGET	SPITFIRE	NOTES
1958	8,729			
1959	21,566			
1960	18,648			Innocenti: estimated 372
1961	10,064	7,656		Innocenti: estimated 2,628
1962	12,041	9,906	1,355	Innocenti: estimated 2,160
1963	8,852	7,625	20,950	Innocenti: estimated 2,232
1964	11,157	11,450	23,387	Innocenti: estimated 288-plus?
1965	8,882	9,162	19,966	
1966	7,024	6,842	17,077	
1967	6,895	7,854	15,235	
1968	7,049	7,272	19,599	
1969	6,136	12,965	18,574	
1970	1,282	15,106	17,041	
1971	1,022	16,469	20,577	
1972		16,243	19,756	
1973		14,048	15,689	
1974		12,443	13,999	
1975		14,478	15,591	
1976		16,879	18,909	
1977		14,329	17,716	
1978		14,312	21,189	
1979		9,778	10,276	
1980			7,456	
Total	129,347	224,817	314,342	

Total, Sprite and Midget: 354,164
Total, Sprite and Midget *less* Sprite Mark I: 305,177
Innocenti, estimated total to 1970: at least 15,000

'Eternal Rivals...'

(Comparison of total prices for Sprite, Midget and Triumph Spitfire year by year – prices quoted for January each year, including Purchase Tax, or Car Tax and VAT, to nearest whole Pound)

YEAR	SPRITE	MIDGET	SPITFIRE	NOTES
1959	£669			
1960	£631			
1961	£631			
1962	£675	£689		
1963	£587	£599	£641	Spitfire introduced October 1962
1964	£587	£599	£641	
1965	£612	£623	£642	
1966	£612	£623	£666	Spitfire Mark II from March 1965
1967	£672	£684	£678	

YEAR	SPRITE	MIDGET	SPITFIRE	NOTES
1968	£672	£684	£717	Spitfire Mark III from March 1967
1969	£756	£769	£780	
1970	£818	£818	£829	
1971	£924	£924	£985	Spitfire Mark IV from November 1970
1972		£928	£982	
1973		£1,003	£1,053	
1974		£1,033	£1,132	
1975		£1,351	£1,360	Spitfire 1500 from December 1974
1976		£1,722	£1,954	
1977		£2,060	£2,359	
1978		£2,221	£2,526	
1979		£2,802	£3,246	
1980		£3,604	£4,064	
1981		£3,821	£4,524	Spitfire production stopped August 1980

Austin-Healey Sprite – Chronology of Chassis Numbers

Date	Chassis number	Notes
March 1958	AN5/501	First Mark I
January 1959	AN5/8927	
January 1960	AN5/30215	
November 1960	AN5/49584	Last built-up car
January 1961	AN5/49821	
February 1961	AN5/50116	Last CKD chassis number
March 1961	H-AN6/101	First Mark II
January 1962	H-AN6/12247	
October 1962	H-AN7/24732	First Mark II, 1,098cc
January 1963	H-AN7/26622	
January 1964	H-AN7/37735	
March 1964	H-AN8/38829	First Mark III
January 1965	H-AN8/48873	
January 1966	H-AN8/57945	
October 1966	H-AN9/64756	First Mark IV
January 1967	H-AN9/64965	
November 1967	H-AN9/72034	Introduction of special North American model
January 1968	H-AN9/72163	
January 1969	H-AN9/79236	
August 1969	H-AN10/85287	First 1970 model, H-AN10
January 1970	H-AN10/85410	
October 1970	H-AN10/86190	Last 1970 model, followed by a break in the numbers
October 1970	H-AN10/86301	First 1971 model
January 1971	A-AN10/86803	First Austin Sprite, A-AN10
July 1971	A-AN10/87824	Model discontinued

Note   First chassis number quoted for each calendar year is approximate.

MG Midget – Chronology of Chassis Numbers

Date	Chassis number	Notes
March 1961	G-AN1/101	First Mark I
January 1962	G-AN1/7526	
October 1962	G-AN2/16184	First Mark I, 1,098cc
January 1963	G-AN2/17688	
January 1964	G-AN2/25361	
March 1964	G-AN3/25788	First Mark II
January 1965	G-AN3/36791	
January 1966	G-AN3/45860	
October 1966	G-AN4/52390	First Mark III
January 1967	G-AN4/52798	
November 1967	G-AN4/60441	Introduction of special North American model
January 1968	G-AN4/60871	
January 1969	G-AN4/67989	
August 1969	G-AN5/74886	First 1970 model, G-AN5
January 1970	G-AN5/81049	
	G-AN5/88596	Last 1970 model, followed by a break in the numbers
July 1970	G-AN5/89501	First 1971 model
January 1971	G-AN5/96853	
	G-AN5/105146	Last 1971 model, followed by a break in the numbers
August 1971	G-AN5/105501	First 1972 model (round-arch)
January 1972	G-AN5/113617	
	G-AN5/123644	Last 1972 model, followed by a break in the numbers
August 1972	G-AN5/123731	First 1973 model
January 1973	G-AN5/129951	
	G-AN5/138753	Last 1973 model, followed by a break in the numbers
August 1973	G-AN5/138801	First 1974 model
January 1974	G-AN5/144039	
	G-AN5/153920	Last 1974 model (last round-arch Mark III), followed by a break in the numbers
October 1974	G-AN6/154101	First Midget 1500 (rubber-bumper), 1975 model
January 1975	G-AN6/156670	
	G-AN6/166193	Last 1975 model, followed by a break in the numbers
August 1975	G-AN6/166301	First 1976 model
January 1976	G-AN6/171356	
	G-AN6/181663	Last 1976 model, followed by a break in the numbers
August 1976	G-AN6/182001	First '1976½' model
December 1976	G-AN6/187529	Last '1976½' model, followed by a break in the numbers
December 1976	G-AN6/188001	First 1977 model
January 1977	G-AN6/188820	
	G-AN6/198804	Last 1977 model, followed by a break in the numbers
August 1977	G-AN6/200001	First 1978 model
January 1978	G-AN6/204350	
	G-AN6/210870	Last 1978 model, followed by a break in the numbers
May 1978	G-AN6/212001	First 1979 model
January 1979	G-AN6/219817	
November 1979	G-AN6/229526	Model discontinued

Note First chassis number quoted for each calendar year is approximate.

Austin-Healey Sprite and MG Midget, Summary of Engine Types

ENGINE TYPE	CAPACITY	USED IN MODEL	PRODUCTION PERIOD	NOTES
9C-U-H	948cc	Sprite Mark I AN5	1958–1961	Mechanical fuel pump, 1⅛in carburettors
9CG-DA-H	948cc	Sprite Mark II H-AN6, Midget Mark I G-AN1	1961–1962	1¼in carburettors
10CG-DA-H	1,098cc	Sprite Mark II H-AN7, Midget Mark I G-AN2	1962–1964	
10CC-DA-H	1,098cc	Sprite Mark III H-AN8, Midget Mark II G-AN3	1964–1966	2in (50mm) main bearings, electric fuel pump
12CC-DA-H	1,275cc	Sprite Mark IV H-AN9, Midget Mark III G-AN4	1966–1967	
12CD-DA-H	1,275cc	Sprite Mark IV H-AN9-U, Midget Mark III G-AN4-U and G-AN5-U	1967–1970	First emissions control engine; for North America only
12CE-DA-H	1,275cc	Sprite Mark IV H-AN9, H-AN10, A-AN10; Midget Mark III G-AN4 and G-AN5	1967–1971	Not for North America
12CJ-DA-H	1,275cc	Midget Mark III G-AN5-U	1970–1971	Evaporative loss control engine; for North America only
12V-586-F-H	1,275cc	Midget Mark III G-AN5	1971–1972	Not for North America
12V-587-Z-L	1,275cc	Midget Mark III G-AN5-U	1971–1972	Low compression; for North America only
12V-588-F-H	1,275cc	Midget Mark III G-AN5	1972–1973	Alternator; not for North America
12V-671-Z-L	1,275cc	Midget Mark III G-AN5-U	1972–1974	Low compression; for North America only
12V-778-F-H	1,275cc	Midget Mark III G-AN5	1973–1974	Not for North America
FP/…-E	1,493cc	Midget 1500 G-AN6	1974–1979	Triumph engine; two SU carburettors
FP/…-UE	1,493cc	Midget 1500 G-AN6-U	1974–1979	Single Zenith–Stromberg carburettor; with catalyst from 1977 onwards; for North America, except California
FP/…-UCE	1,493cc	Midget 1500 G-AN6-U	1975–1979	Californian specification engine, always fitted with catalyst

Appendix 2

Notes to Production Figure Tables

Abbreviations:

RHD, H = Right-Hand Drive, Home market
RHD, E = Right-Hand Drive, Export
LHD, E = Left-Hand Drive, Export
LNA, E = Left-hand drive for North America, Export
CKD, R = Completely Knocked Down exports, Right-hand drive
CKD, L = Completely Knocked Down exports, Left-hand drive

The figures in these tables have been based on figures compiled in the MG factory at Abingdon at the time of production, with some corrections for known inaccuracies and errors. The original production records are now kept in the archives of the British Motor Industry Heritage Trust (BMIHT), and are reproduced here courtesy of the BMIHT.

PRODUCTION FIGURES – AUSTIN-HEALEY SPRITE

AN5, Mark I Frog-eye

Year	RHD,H	RHD,E	LHD,E	LNA,E	CKD,R	CKD,L	Total	Innocenti
1958	1,927	706		5,898	169	29	8,729	
1959	4,042	396		16,908	220	0	21,566	
1960	3,972	339		13,441	872	24	18,648	372
1961					44	0	44	252
Total	9,941	1,441		36,247	1,305	53	48,987	624

Note 5 cars missing of total potential build by chassis number series, including Innocentis.

H-AN6, Mark II (948cc)

Year	RHD,H	RHD,E	LHD,E	LNA,E	CKD,R	Total	Innocenti
1961	1,607	295		8,028	90	10,020	2,376
1962	1,989	205		8,000	236	10,430	1,800
Total	3,596	500	3,214	12,814	326	20,450	4,176

Note There were also 5 special race cars built in 1961–1962, for Sebring.

H-AN7, Mark II (1,098cc)

Year	RHD,H	RHD,E	LHD,E	LNA,E	CKD,R	Total	Innocenti
1962	179	48	251	989	144	1,611	360
1963	1,400	149	1,523	5,064	716	8,852	2,232
1964	31	8	9	588	116	752	288
Total	1,610	205	1,783	6,641	976	11,215	2,880

Note Plus 1 or 2 development cars built during 1963.

H-AN8, Mark III (1,098cc)

Year	RHD,H	RHD,E	LHD,E	LNA,E	CKD,R	Total
1964	1,773	147	1,315	6,562	608	10,405
1965	2,209	159	775	5,095	644	8,882
1966	1,143	97	332	4,902	144	6,618
Total	5,125	403	2,422	16,559	1,396	25,905

Note And 1 car which has not been found or identified in the records.

H-AN9, Mark IV (1,275cc)

Year	RHD,H	RHD,E	LHD,E	LNA,E	Total
1966	352	5	37	12	406
1967	1,270	83	339	5,203	6,895
1968	1,005	38	164	5,842	7,049
1969	900	34	94	4,979	6,007
Total	3,527	160	634	16,036	20,357

Note The 1967 and total figures include the 489 cars which were built at Cowley rather than Abingdon during 1967. Another 190 chassis numbers which had been allocated to Cowley were in fact not used on cars in production.

H-AN10, Mark IV (1,275cc)

Year	RHD,H	Total
1969	129	129
1970	1,282	1,282
Total	1,411	1,411

Note There was a gap of 110 chassis numbers unused between 1970 and 1971 model years.

A-AN10, Austin Sprite (1,275cc)

Year	RHD,H	Total
1971	1,022	1,022
Total	1,022	1,022

Model by Model

AN5	48,987 (plus Innocenti: 624)
H-AN6	20,450 (plus Innocenti: 4,176)
H-AN7	11,215 (plus Innocenti: 2,880)
H-AN8	25,905
H-AN9	20,357
H-AN10	1,411
A-AN10	1,022

Total	129,347 (plus Innocenti: 7,680)

PRODUCTION FIGURES – MG MIDGET

G-AN1, Mark I (948cc)

Year	RHD,H	RHD,E	LHD,E	LNA,E	CKD,R	CKD,L	Total
1961	1,124	266	1,353	4,889	24		7,656
1962	2,295	498	1,727	3,832	24	48	8,424
Total	3,419	764	3,080	8,721	48	48	16,080

G-AN2, Mark I (1,098cc)

Year	RHD,H	RHD,E	LHD,E	LNA,E	CKD,R	CKD,L	Total
1962	288	114	384	678	6	12	1,482
1963	2,066	313	1,654	3,562	30		7,625
1964	140	10	1	337	6		494
Total	2,494	437	2,039	4,577	42	12	9,601

G-AN3, Mark II (1,098cc)

Year	RHD,H	RHD,E	LHD,E	LNA,E	CKD,R	Total
1964	3,061	340	1,695	5,830	30	10,956
1965	3,626	278	844	4,390	24	9,162
1966	2,597	131	516	3,215	24	6,483
Total	9,284	749	3,055	13,435	78	26,601

G-AN4, Mark III (1,275cc)

Year	RHD,H	RHD,E	LHD,E	LNA,E	CKD,R	Total
1966	291	17	15	36	0	359
1967	2,853	169	470	4,102	260	7,854
1968	1,790	96	235	4,687	464	7,272
1969	1,726	71	139	4,930	64	6,930
Total	6,660	353	859	13,755	788	22,415

Note The 1967 and total figures include the 476 cars which were built at Cowley rather than Abingdon during 1967.

G-AN5, Mark III (1,275cc), square arch

Year	RHD,H	RHD,E	LHD,E	LNA,E	CKD,R	Total
1969	1,196	154		4,605	80	6,035
1970	3,392	536		10,970	208	15,106
1971	1,657	180		6,458	108	8,403
Total	6,245	870		22,033	396	29,544

Note From 1969 onwards, non-North American export cars were counted together, regardless of whether they had RHD or LHD.

G-AN5, Mark III (1,275cc), round arch

Year	RHD,H	RHD,E	LHD,E	LNA,E	Total
1971	430	83		7,553	8,066
1972	4,635	92		11,516	16,243
1973	3,737			10,311	14,048
1974	1,508			8,422	9,930
Total	10,310	175		37,802	48,287

Note Production of CKD cars for Australia ceased in 1971. Production of non-North American export cars appears to have ceased in 1972.

G-AN6, Midget 1500

Year	RHD,H	LNA,E	Total
1974	591	1,922	2,513
1975	2,531	11,947	14,478
1976	3,465	13,414	16,879
1977	3,774	10,555	14,329
1978	4,574	9,738	14,312
1979	2,912	6,866	9,778
Total	17,847	54,442	72,289

Model by Model

G-AN1	16,080
G-AN2	9,601
G-AN3	26,601
G-AN4	22,415
G-AN5	29,544 (square arch)
G-AN5	48,287 (round arch)
G-AN6	72,289
Total	224,817

Note The 1500 model appears to have been built only to either home market specification with RHD, or to North American export specification with LHD.

Index